ANCIENT ROME IN 30 SECONDS

First published in the UK in 2016 by
Ivy Kids
Ovest House
58 West Street
Brighton BN1 2RA
United Kingdom
www.quartoknows.com

British Library Cataloguing-in-Publication Data.
A catalogue record for this book is available from the British Library

ISBN: 978-1-78240-398-2

This book was conceived, designed and produced by
Ivy Kids

PUBLISHER Susan Kelly
CREATIVE DIRECTOR Michael Whitehead
COMMISSIONING EDITOR Hazel Songhurst
MANAGING EDITOR Susie Behar
PROJECT EDITOR Liz Wyse
ART DIRECTOR Hanri van Wyk
DESIGNER Emily Portnoi
EDITORIAL ASSISTANT Lucy Menzies
DESIGN ASSISTANT Emily Hurlock
BLACK AND WHITE ILLUSTRATIONS Jack Xander

Printed in China

1 3 5 7 9 10 8 6 4 2

ANCIENT ROME
IN 30 SECONDS

SIMON HOLLAND

ILLUSTRATED BY ADAM HILL
CONSULTANT: DR. MATTHEW NICHOLLS

IVY KIDS

Contents

About this book

... in 60 seconds

The Romans are among history's greatest superstars. They were world-famous in their day, and they're still famous now. Their huge empire may have ended hundreds of years ago, but their ideas, inventions and ways of life live on. In fact, you probably already know more about the Romans than you realise...

When you think about the Roman world, you might picture a gory gladiator fight or a bloodthirsty battle, noble emperors or mysterious gods and goddesses. And you would be right – the Romans had all of this and more. Ancient Rome was an amazing civilization with ideas about daily life, technology, culture and politics that, to us, seem way ahead of their time.

The Roman civilization spanned more than 2,000 years and reached out far and wide across the world – so how did they manage this incredible feat?

For a start, they introduced ideas from other cultures into their society. They also believed that their ways of life were the best, and – helped by their awesome legions – they set out on a mission to bring as many nations as possible into one huge empire.

Evidence of the Roman world still exists. Many buildings, statues, coins, pottery, mosaics and jewellery items have survived, along with poetry, plays, documents and letters. Not only this – every time you turn on a tap, look at a calendar, visit the leisure centre, or travel down a long, straight road you are experiencing a way of life that began long ago in Ancient Rome.

In this book, every topic is covered in one page, which you can read as fast or as slow as you like. If you're in a real hurry, there's a speedy 3-second sum-up to read instead! There's also a full-colour picture for an at-a-glance guide. Then, if you have a spare few minutes, there are lots of extra facts to discover and hands-on activities to try.

Here come the Romans

The great Roman civilization, which ruled Europe for hundreds of years, started life as a few scattered farming settlements. Slowly, Rome grew into a huge, bustling city with temples, great monuments and public arenas. Early on it was governed as a 'republic', with power held by the people, but by 27 BCE the Republic had been overthrown and Augustus became the first Roman emperor. At its peak, the mighty Roman Empire ruled most of Europe and the Mediterranean region.

Glossary

aristocrat A member of the ruling class of Ancient Rome. Aristocrats passed on their wealth and position to their children.

Carthaginians Based in the city of Carthage in northern Africa (modern Tunisia), the Carthaginian people dominated much of the Mediterranean with their powerful navy from c. 650 to 146 BCE.

citizen A person in Ancient Rome who had certain rights, including the right to elect officials, own property and hold office.

civil war A war between different groups within the same country.

conquer To defeat or overcome an enemy, usually by using force.

consul The leader of the republican government in Rome. Two consuls were elected, who served for just one year. Each had the right to 'veto' (say no) to the other's decisions.

emperor The supreme leader of the Roman Empire. Sometimes, the emperor was even thought of as a god.

Empire Either the post-**republican** period in Rome's history, when it was ruled by an **emperor**, or the territory conquered and administered by Rome.

government A group of people who make and administer a country's or territory's laws.

kingdom A country, state or territory that is ruled by a king or a queen.

magistrate An official who was elected by the citizens of Rome to serve the Roman government. When Rome was a republic, the **Senate** issued advice to the magistrates, who discussed it and decided whether or not to act on it.

migration The movement of peoples from one place to another, often crossing political or state boundaries.

oratory The art of public speaking, often seen in the **Senate**, where individuals set out to persuade their fellow citizens to follow their ideas.

republic A form of government that allowed the people to elect officials, rather than be governed by a king. The Roman Republic is a model for many forms of government today.

Senate A governing body, which was made up of important or wealthy members of Roman society. The Senate's role was to debate policy, propose new laws and offer advice to elected officials.

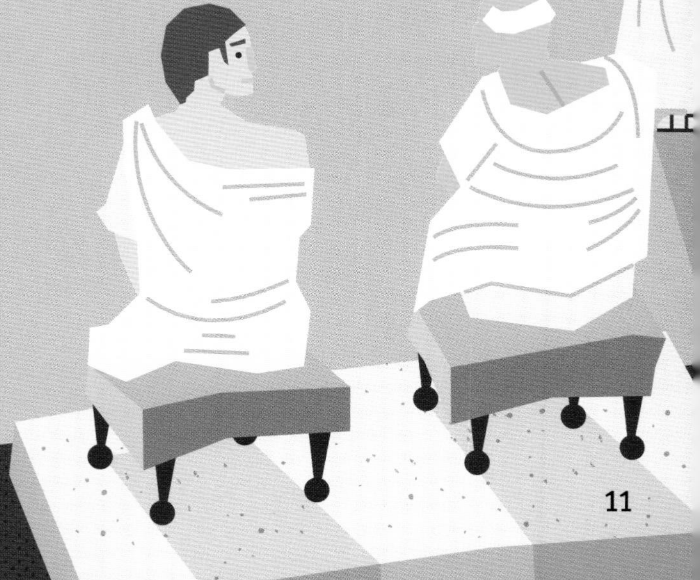

Roots of Rome

... in 30 seconds

The history of Rome goes back perhaps as far as 1000 BCE when farming settlements started to appear in this part of central Italy. There were many hills in the area, and settlements on two of them – the Palatine Hill and Capitoline Hill – grew to become a central part of Rome. There were other settlements in the area, too, so they may all have come together to form a small kingdom, possibly from around 625 BCE.

These farming people were known as Latins. Other people, like the Etruscans, who arrived in the area between 650 and 600 BCE, also lived there.

The Etruscans had probably come from the eastern Mediterranean in around 1000 BCE. They organized their towns into city-states, each one ruled by a king, and this civilization had a big influence on the development of early Rome. Some of Rome's first kings were Etruscan. They were the brains behind some important buildings such as the Capitoline temple and the Cloaca Maxima (the main sewage drain).

3-second sum-up

Legend says that Rome was founded by Romulus, but it probably grew from a cluster of farming settlements.

A Roman legend

Romans believed that the city of Rome was created by the sons of a god. Romulus and Remus were twin sons of Mars, the god of war. As babies, they were left in a basket on the River Tiber. When the basket ran aground, the twins were discovered by a she-wolf that, along with a woodpecker, fed them, before a shepherd found them and took them in. When they grew up, the brothers decided to build a city, but disagreed over where to build it. Romulus killed Remus and named his city – Rome – after himself.

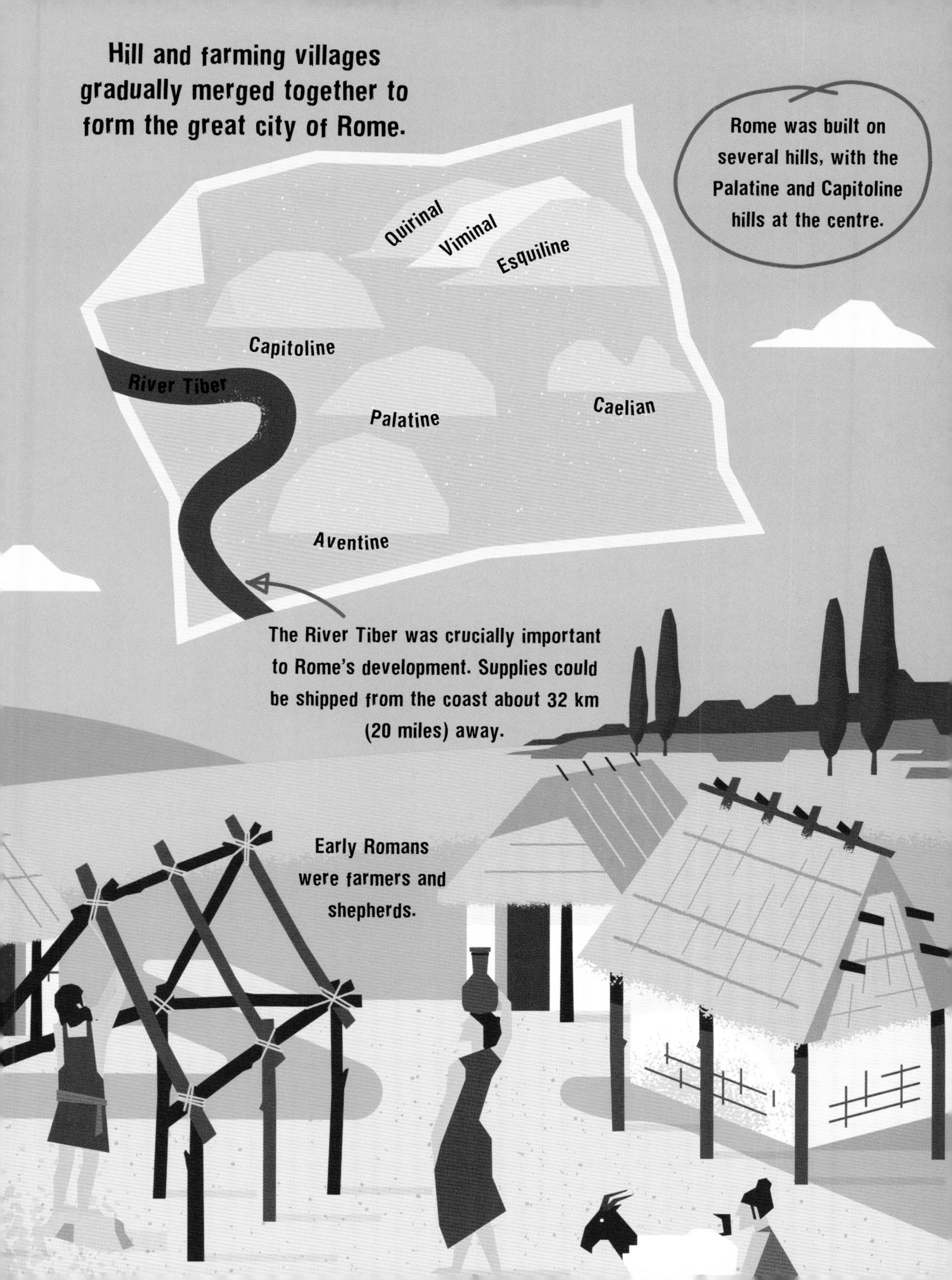
Hill and farming villages gradually merged together to form the great city of Rome.
Rome was built on several hills, with the Palatine and Capitoline hills at the centre.
Quirinal
Viminal
Esquiline
Capitoline
River Tiber
Palatine
Caelian
Aventine
The River Tiber was crucially important to Rome's development. Supplies could be shipped from the coast about 32 km (20 miles) away.
Early Romans were farmers and shepherds.

The Republic

... in 30 seconds

Rome was originally ruled by a king elected by the people. The first six kings ruled well; they built temples and city walls, set up chariot races and boxing competitions for the public to enjoy, and expanded the kingdom by conquering nearby lands.

But the seventh king, Tarquin the Proud – who came to power in 535 BCE – used force to keep the people under his control. A ruthless tyrant, he believed he and his family were above the law. So, in 509 BCE, Tarquin was overthrown and the Romans began to make their land into a 'republic', a system in which power is held by the people instead of a king.

The Roman Republic was firmly in place within 200 years. The people chose officials as their representatives to run the state and make decisions. These officials were called magistrates, and they were advised by a small number of aristocrats (from rich, powerful families) who made up the Senate. A senator's job was for life. The Senate controlled state spending, Rome's rule of its empire, and advised the magistrates.

The Senate was led by two chief magistrates, or 'consuls'. These consuls served for just one year, to prevent them from becoming too powerful.

3-second sum-up

Rome became a republic, governed by the Senate.

The Senate

The members of the Senate weren't directly elected by the people. They were chosen by important Romans. Their role was to discuss the political issues of the state and give out written decrees – or official bits of advice – for the magistrates and consuls to follow when waging wars or spending public money. The Senate was often a rowdy place, full of speeches interrupted by shouts, boos and arguments about how money was to be spent!

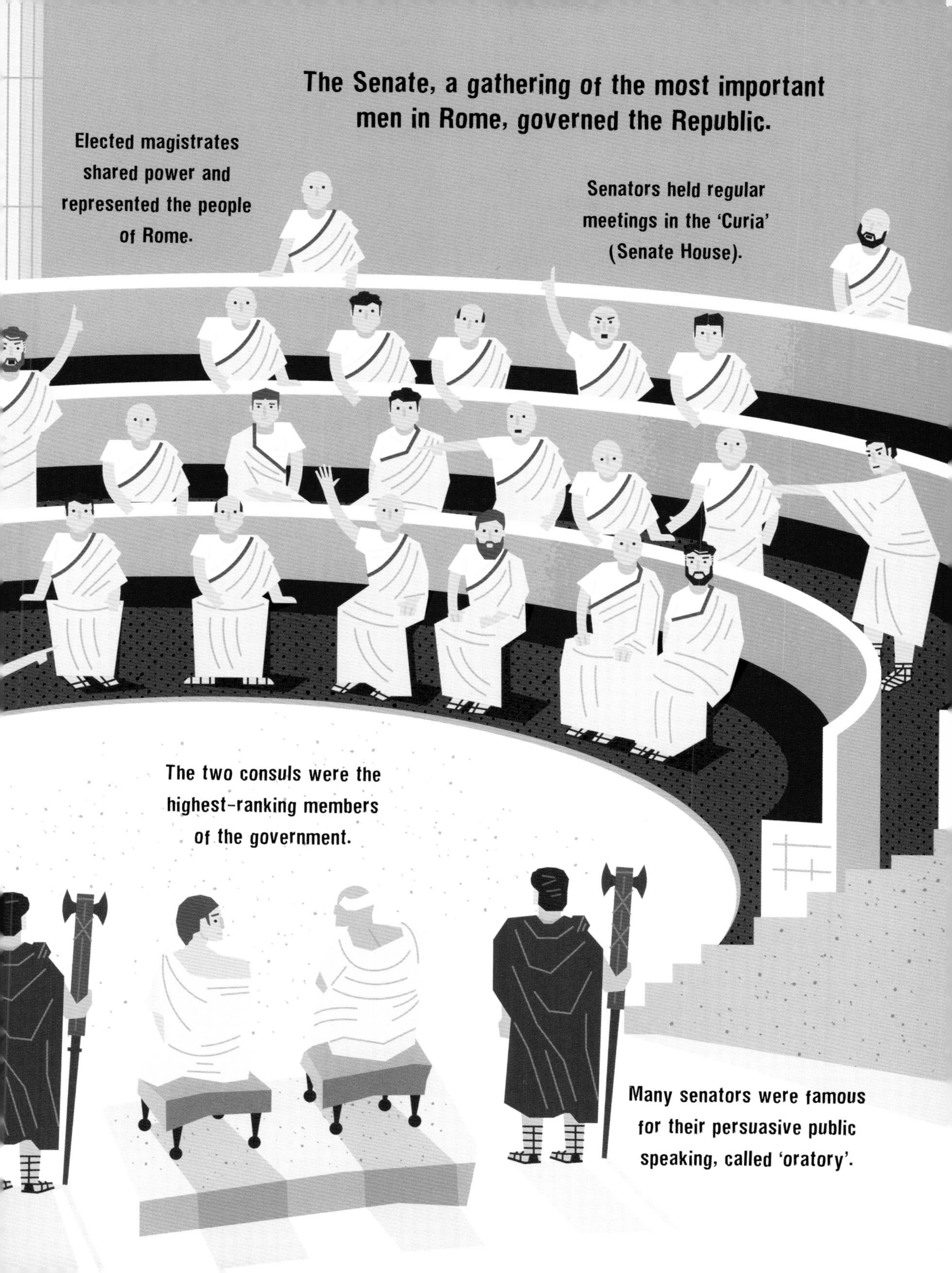

The Senate, a gathering of the most important men in Rome, governed the Republic.

Elected magistrates shared power and represented the people of Rome.

Senators held regular meetings in the 'Curia' (Senate House).

The two consuls were the highest-ranking members of the government.

Many senators were famous for their persuasive public speaking, called 'oratory'.

Start of an empire

... in 30 seconds

By the 1st century BCE, Rome had taken over most of Italy, and had won more land from neighbouring countries. Further territory was gained after battles against the mighty Carthaginians of northern Africa and the Macedonians of Greece and the Middle East.

However, fierce power struggles broke out between top-ranking Romans, leading to civil war. In 45 BCE, a general named Julius Caesar led his army against the forces of his great rival, Pompey. Caesar won, but his arrogance and hunger for power alarmed many Romans. In 44 BCE, Caesar was brutally murdered by a group of his fellow senators.

After Caesar's death, Mark Antony, who was one of Caesar's supporters, agreed to govern Rome with Caesar's great-nephew, Octavian. But Octavian and Antony soon became rivals, too. In 31 BCE, Octavian defeated Antony at the Battle of Actium, off the west coast of Greece.

The power struggles and fighting brought the Republic to an end. Octavian later took the name Caesar Augustus. In 27 BCE, he became Rome's first emperor. This paved the way towards a different kind of government that had one extremely powerful person in charge.

3-second sum-up

Power struggles between powerful Romans brought an end to the Republic.

Assassinated!

After his victory over Pompey, Julius Caesar (100–44 BCE) set himself up as a dictator in Rome, taking all of the power for himself. A group of high-ranking senators feared that this would destroy the Republic. On 15 March, 44 BCE, a group of senators attacked Caesar during a debate. They used concealed daggers, and stabbed him 23 times. This dramatic event plunged Rome into panic and confusion.

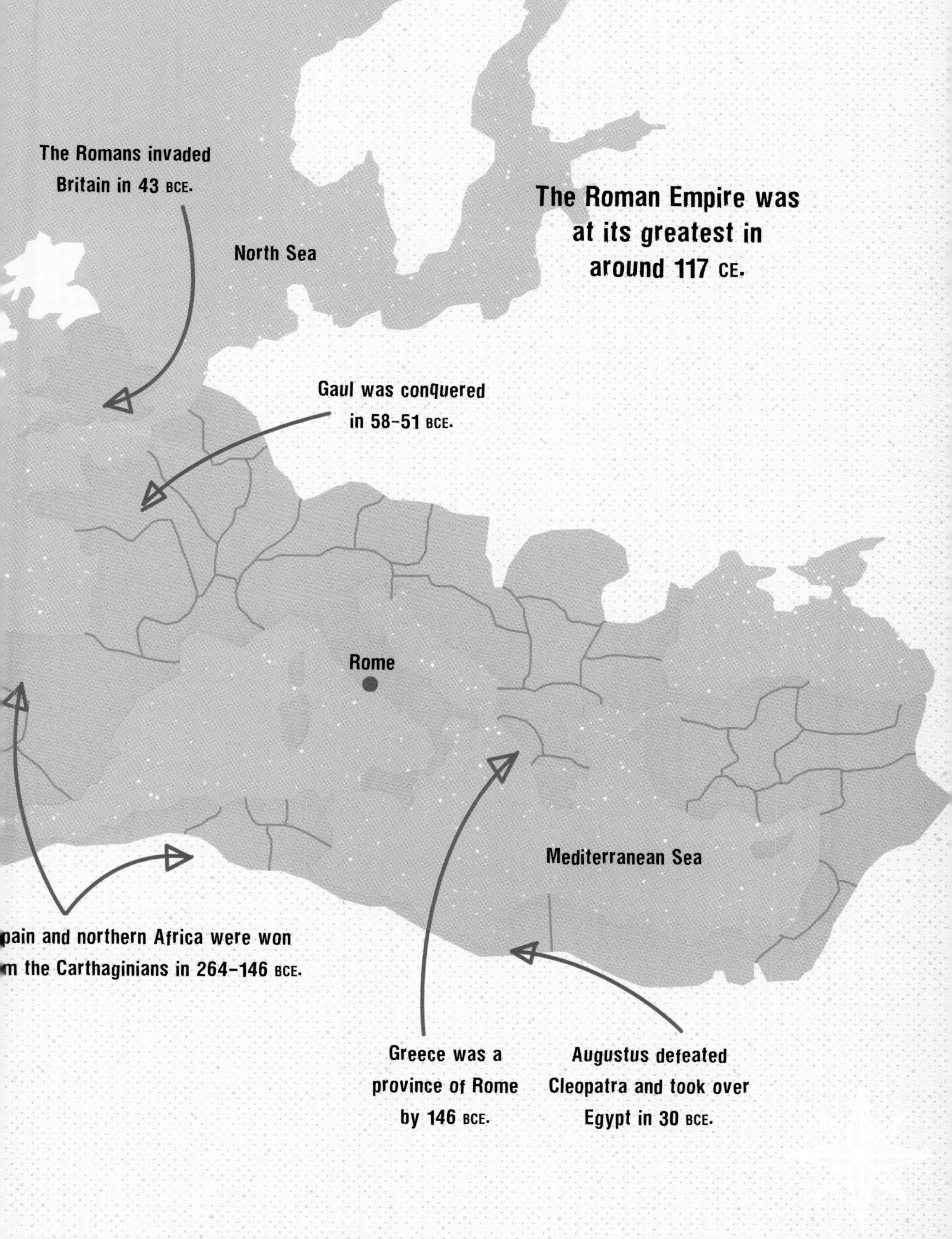

The Romans invaded Britain in 43 BCE.
North Sea
The Roman Empire was at its greatest in around 117 CE.
Gaul was conquered in 58–51 BCE.
Rome
pain and northern Africa were won
m the Carthaginians in 264–146 BCE.
Mediterranean Sea
Greece was a province of Rome by 146 BCE.
Augustus defeated Cleopatra and took over Egypt in 30 BCE.

The emperors

... in 30 seconds

From the time of Caesar Augustus until the end of the Eastern Roman Empire in 1453, over 250 men served as emperors and co-emperors. Some of them were terrible leaders and many didn't stay in power for long – but some became great generals or inspiring emperors.

With power firmly in their hands, many emperors were able to act in any way they chose – good or bad! Early emperors, such as Claudius and Trajan, focused on expanding and protecting the Empire, conquering other nations and bringing them into the Roman way of life, which the Romans believed was the 'right' and 'best' way to live.

However, some emperors used their power badly. Gaius – nicknamed 'Caligula' – was a true tyrant. At first, he was popular, but this was probably because he spent huge sums of money on games and entertainment for the common people. However, he became more and more thirsty for power and insisted on being treated as a god. People who looked at his balding head as he walked by could be put to death, and he even wanted to make his horse a consul! He was assassinated at the age of 29.

3-second sum-up

The emperors had complete power. Some are still famous today for their actions.

3-minute mission Be an emperor

You need: • A pen or pencil • Paper

Some emperors were bold, decisive, intelligent – and fair. Others were weak or tyrannical. But what kind of emperor would YOU make? If you ruled your house, what would your main commandments be? Write a list of ten policies (political ideas) for the management of your Home Empire.

The Roman emperors we still talk about are those who made the Empire strong through their actions – or those who were cruel tyrants.

Caesar Augustus (27 BCE–14 CE)

The first Roman emperor, who used his strong army to bring peace and stability.

Caligula (37–41 CE)

He ignored the Senate, spent lavishly and insisted he was a god.

Trajan (98–117 CE)

The Empire reached its greatest extent under Trajan, the 'great conqueror'.

Constantine (306–337 CE)

The first Christian emperor, he moved his capital to Byzantium (Constantinople).

Nero (54–68 CE)

A brutal leader, he had his enemies executed, including his own wife!

Diocletian (284–305 CE)

He strengthened the weakened Empire by dividing it into four regions with separate rulers.

Romans at war

However big the Empire grew, the ambitious Romans were always trying to make it bigger. Their well-trained army was the best around and it was helped by powerful war machines. Battles fought against the Carthaginians, the German tribes and others gave Rome control of a huge sweep of land stretching from Britain to North Africa. To defend this newly conquered land, the Romans erected a network of forts along the borders of their vast territories.

Romans at war

Glossary

ballista A kind of giant crossbow, used for firing either arrows or stone balls at fortifications.

battering ram A large, heavy log with an iron head that was used to batter and break down walls and gateways.

border A division between land belonging to the Roman Empire and another territory.

cavalry A troop of 120 men who served as scouts (lookouts) and messengers, and who were attached to each Roman legion.

century A group of 80 soldiers, made up of ten groups of eight.

citizen A person in Ancient Rome who had certain rights, including the right to elect officials, own property and hold office.

cohort Six centuries of 80 men formed a cohort.

formations The pre-planned movements and positions used by the well-trained Roman army.

fort The well-defended living quarters of Roman soldiers, where they lived and trained before going out on a campaign.

Gauls The Celtic tribespeople who lived in what is now France. They were warriors and farmers, who defended their territory against Roman invasion but were conquered by Julius Caesar in 52 BCE.

imperial Relating to an empire.

legionary A soldier aged under 45, who was a Roman **citizen**.

missile An object that is forcibly thrown at a target, either by hand or from a mechanical weapon.

onager A giant catapult, which used a sling to fire rocks through walls and fortifications.

salary An amount of money paid at regular intervals in exchange for work or service.

siege When an enemy position is surrounded to ensure that no supplies reach the people trapped within.

siege tower A tower mounted on wheels, which could be moved close to enemy fortifications. From here, soldiers could use a **ballista** to fire arrows over defensive walls, and use **battering rams** to break down walls and gates.

An imperial army

... in 30 seconds

The Romans were extremely successful on the battlefield, even though the ancient world was full of great armies and fierce warriors such as the Carthaginians, Macedonians and Gauls. This was because their soldiers were well trained and disciplined, and the army was better organized than their enemies' fighting forces.

Roman soldiers were known as 'legionaries' because they were grouped into huge 'legions' of up to 6,000 men, including officers and non-fighting staff such as surgeons. In the 1st century CE, there were around 28 Roman legions serving the Empire – that's 168,000 soldiers!

Legionaries were normally paid fairly well – plus, they could get promoted up through the ranks and receive bonuses in times of military success. Some of their earnings had to be used to pay for their food, as well as for standard kit and weaponry. The word 'salary' comes from 'salarium'. This was the amount given to a Roman soldier to buy salt, an expensive necessity.

Soldiers came from all over Rome's vast empire. Once a soldier had signed up, he had to stay in the army for 25 years.

3-second sum-up

The army was well organized, well trained and disciplined.

Life in the Roman army

THE UPSIDES
- Travel the world
- A good education
- A job for life
- Regular pay, plus 'booty'
- A pension or gift of land on retirement

THE DOWNSIDES
- Harsh punishments
- Dangerous battles
- Tough living conditions
- Women unable to join and no marriage allowed
- Back-breaking physical labour

Each legion consisted of between 5,500 and 6,000 men.

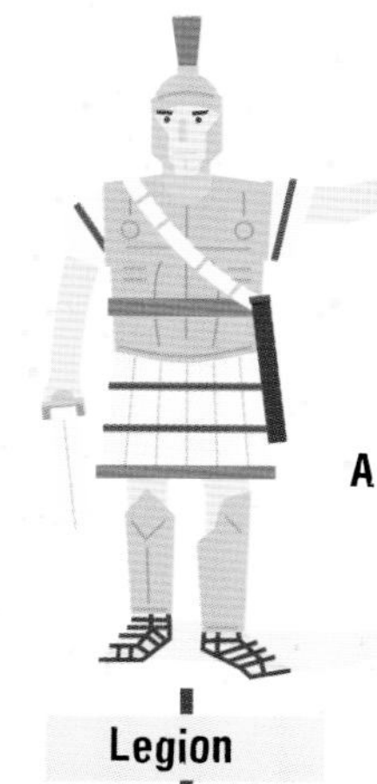

A Legate was in charge of the entire legion.

A Legion was divided into ten large units called cohorts.

Legion

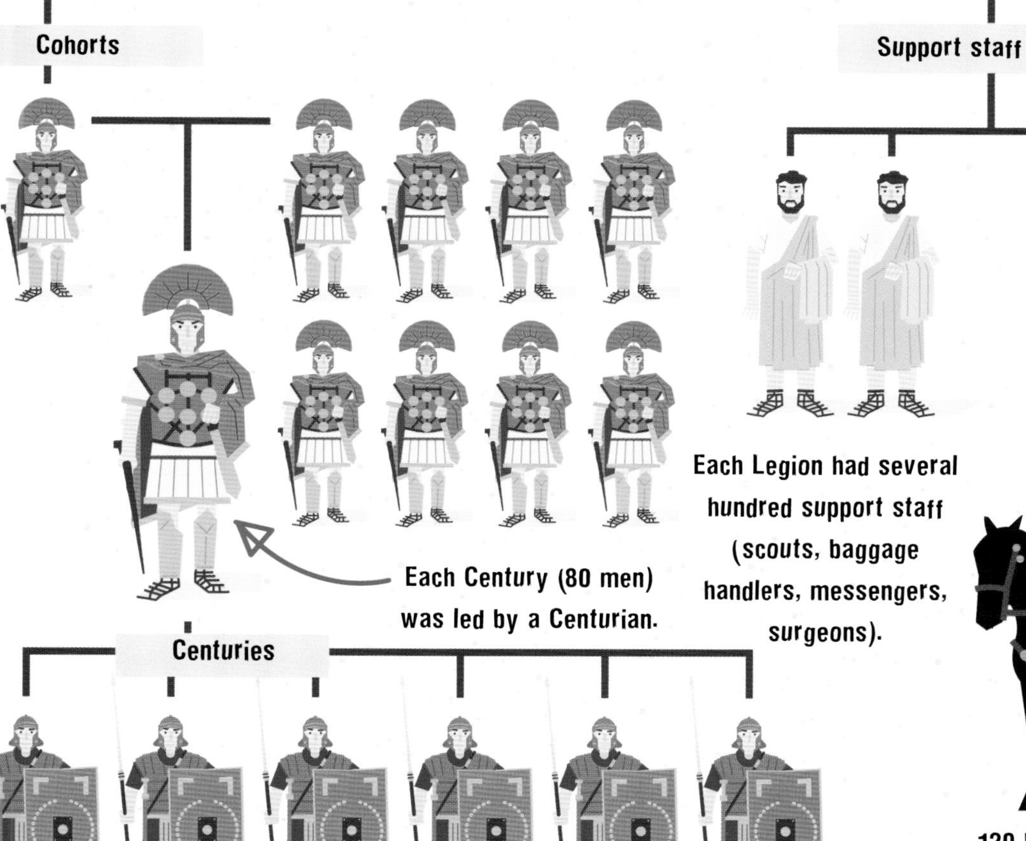

Each Century (80 men) was led by a Centurian.

Each Legion had several hundred support staff (scouts, baggage handlers, messengers, surgeons).

120 horsemen accompanied each Legion.

There were six Centuries in a Cohort, which was made up of 480 men.

Equipped for battle

... in 30 seconds

Being a soldier gave men a good job and a high status in life – but it was hard work. Legionaries marched up to 30 km (20 miles) each day, hauling 40 kg (90 lbs) of heavy equipment such as tents, food, cooking equipment and weapons – plus all of their own personal kit and armour.

Legionaries carried two 'pila' (javelins), to be thrown when charging at the enemy. They also wore a 'gladius' (short sword). This was for close combat – and if it broke or got lost, they'd reach for their 'pugio' (a small dagger). A shield was held on their left arm, while a helmet protected their head.

Soldiers fought in different formations. In the 'testudo' (tortoise) formation, the men overlapped their shields to the sides and above to provide all-round protection. This was useful in battles where weapons might rain down on them from above. The 'wedge', or triangular formation, was designed to barge through lines of enemy troops.

Some legionaries had special skills – there were archers, heavy weapons operators, horsemen (in the cavalry) and swimmers who could get into 'surprise attack' positions.

3-second sum-up

A legionary was trained to respond to different commands in battle, and many had special skills.

3-minute mission Make an imperial shield

You need: • A large sheet of corrugated cardboard • Colouring pens • Coloured paper • Scissors • Sticky tape

1 Cut out a large rectangle from the cardboard, making sure the corrugations run from top to bottom.

2 Create your design using pens or strips of coloured paper.

3 Attach two small strips of card to make a handle on the other side, bending the shield as you go to create a curved shape.

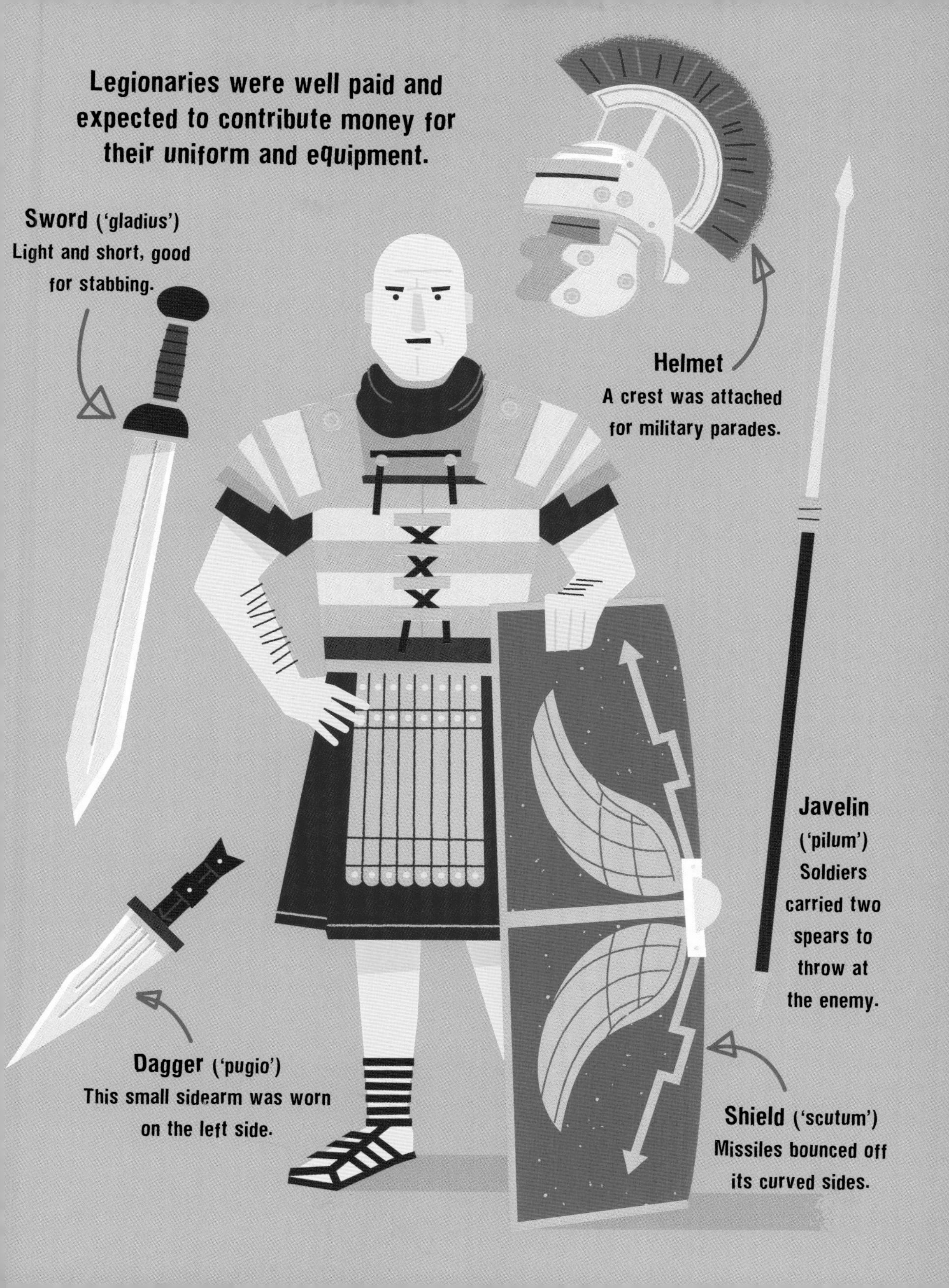
Legionaries were well paid and expected to contribute money for their uniform and equipment.
Sword ('gladius')
Light and short, good for stabbing.
Helmet
A crest was attached for military parades.
Javelin ('pilum')
Soldiers carried two spears to throw at the enemy.
Dagger ('pugio')
This small sidearm was worn on the left side.
Shield ('scutum')
Missiles bounced off its curved sides.

War machines

... in 30 seconds

Legions used an array of powerful war machines to help them expand their territory, crush rebellions or fight enemies on the borders of the Empire. Since Roman military campaigns could carry on for years, their machines had to be built to last.

Some of these machines were 'flat-packed' (like furniture!), so that they could simply be wheeled to the battle on carts and then put together. Others had to be built on-site, which meant the soldiers had to cut down nearby trees to get the wood they needed.

The onager, or 'wild ass', was a giant catapult that fired rocks or balls of burning tar. Its name probably comes from its sudden motion – a bit like the kick of a wild donkey. It could sling objects up to 300 m (984 ft) over the walls of enemy fortifications. The Romans also used the powerful ballista, which was like a wind-up crossbow. It fired stones and spears.

If the legionaries were attacking a fort or city, they would roll tall, wooden 'siege towers' right up to the walls, and use battering rams, ropes, hooks and ladders to force their way through. There was simply no escaping the Roman army!

3-second sum-up

Huge war machines and clever defence formations helped the Romans to attack their enemies and to defend themselves.

3-minute mission Build a mini onager

You need: • 3 lolly sticks • An elastic band • Paper • An adult helper

1 Get your helper to hold two lolly sticks, one in each hand, and stretch an elastic band between them.

2 Poke the third lolly stick between the stretched loop of the band, then turn it around until you can feel the tension build up.

3 Place a scrunched-up paper missile at the end of your lolly stick 'launcher'... then release!

Legions used powerful weapons on the battlefield, and built siege engines to force their way into enemy cities and forts.

Hand-to-hand fighting was brutal. The 'testudo' formation looked like a tortoise shell, and gave legionaries some protection.

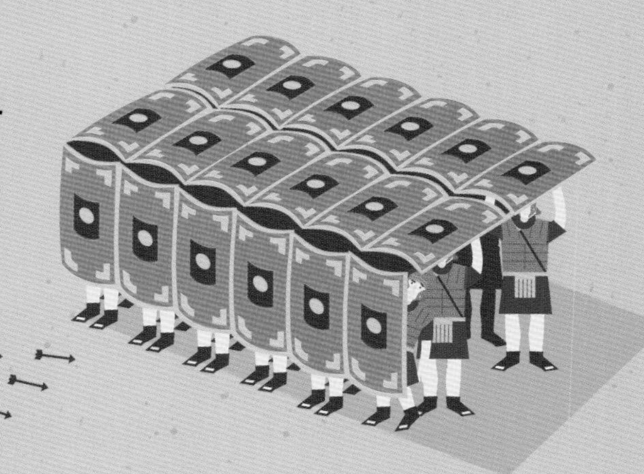

Tall siege towers were rolled up to enemy walls, so that soldiers could fire over the fortifications into the city.

Missiles from the onager could hit a target 300 m (984 ft) away.

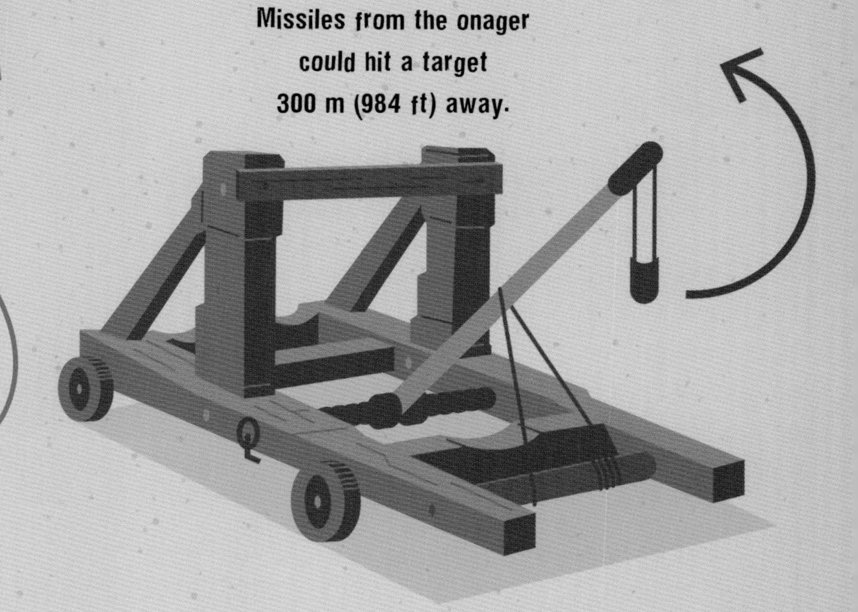

Siege towers and other large weapons were often built on site, as they were incredibly heavy and very difficult to move.

Big battles

... in 30 seconds

The Romans had to fight many battles both on water and on land to remain a powerful force in the ancient world, and they made many enemies in the process.

The lands in and around the Mediterranean Sea were controlled by Carthage, a powerful city-state in northern Africa. From 264 to 146 BCE, the Romans fought three major wars against them, which are known as the Punic Wars (from the Latin 'Punicus', meaning 'Carthaginian'). The Carthaginians' leader was called Hannibal and it is said his father made him swear on his life to forever be an enemy of Rome.

Another great enemy of Rome was a tribe of people called the Huns, who lived in what is now Hungary and Germany. The king of the Huns was called Attila. He gathered together many of the Roman Empire's enemies to fight four massive battles against them.

One of Rome's most notable foes was King Pyrrhus of Epirus, a country in northwestern Greece. He won two big battles against the Romans, but he lost so many men that he didn't want to win any more! A victory won at excessive cost is still called a 'Pyrrhic victory'.

3-second sum-up

Rome had powerful enemies, including the Carthaginians and the Huns, and fought major battle against them.

Hannibal's road to Rome

In 218 BCE, Hannibal wanted to surprise the Romans by attacking them by land instead of by sea, so he led his troops and war elephants across Spain, France and then over the Alps into northern Italy. Hannibal lost about three-quarters of his army and almost all of his elephants in the freezing mountains. Despite this, he spent 15 years attacking northern Italy, and even got to within 5 km (3 miles) of Rome, though he failed to conquer the city. Hannibal lived to fight another day, leading his troops back to Spain.

In the second Punic War (218–204 BCE), the Carthaginian leader, Hannibal, made a daring crossing of the Alps to attack Rome.

Hannibal's route took him from Spain, through Gaul (France) and south into Italy.

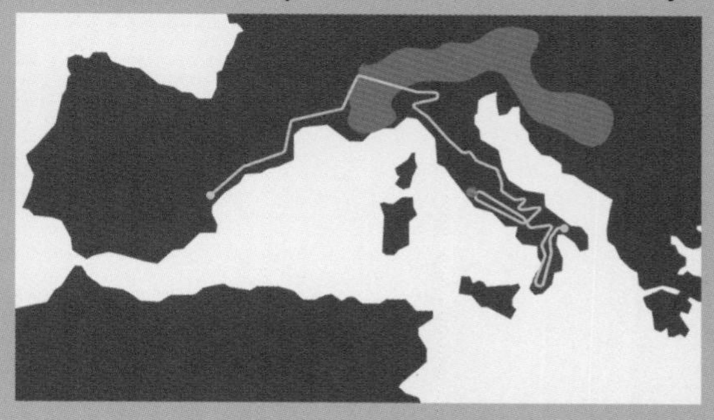

Hannibal wanted to surprise the Romans by attacking them by land instead of sea.

Hannibal started out with 30–40 elephants, but lost most of them on the journey – together with around three-quarters of his men.

Once in Italy, Hannibal defeated the Romans in several battles, but never managed to conquer Rome.

Conquerors abroad

... in 30 seconds

The Romans were always trying to conquer new lands and make their empire bigger. But they had to work hard to win and keep those lands. Along the frontiers of the Empire, they built huge, impressive forts to defend the borders and send out a loud message to all around: 'We are the Romans. Beware – we are extremely powerful!'

Once the forts had been built, they became mini-towns where between 500 and 1,000 soldiers, officers and other army-related people could live and work – doing a wide range of jobs and crafts.

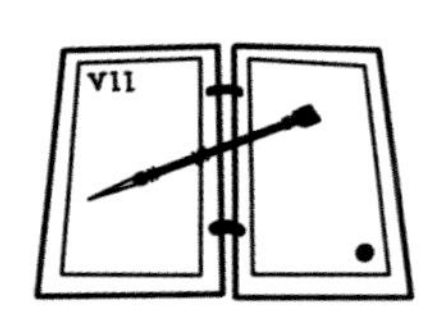

One of the most remote outposts of the Roman Empire was Britain, invaded by the Romans in 43 CE. In 122 CE, the conquerors built Hadrian's Wall across northern Britain, which had 16 forts. The wall marked out the northernmost limit of the Roman Empire, and protected them from attacks by northern tribes.

Life was extremely tough for the soldiers based in Britain. Their letters home reveal how much they missed their families. One soldier asked his family to send warm socks – the bitter northern winters were hard to get used to!

3-second sum-up

Legionaries built frontier forts in the new lands they conquered.

3-minute mission Design a fort

You need: • Plain or graph paper • Pen and pencils • Ruler

Draw a plan for your own fortress town. Think about how you're going to defend it (walls, towers, ditches) and how people will get in and out. How will you lay out the buildings and supplies for the hundreds of soldiers and other people who will live there? Don't forget sleeping quarters, food stores, toilets, and stables for the horses. What sort of people will you need to build your mini town?

Huge military outposts were built at the borders of the Empire.

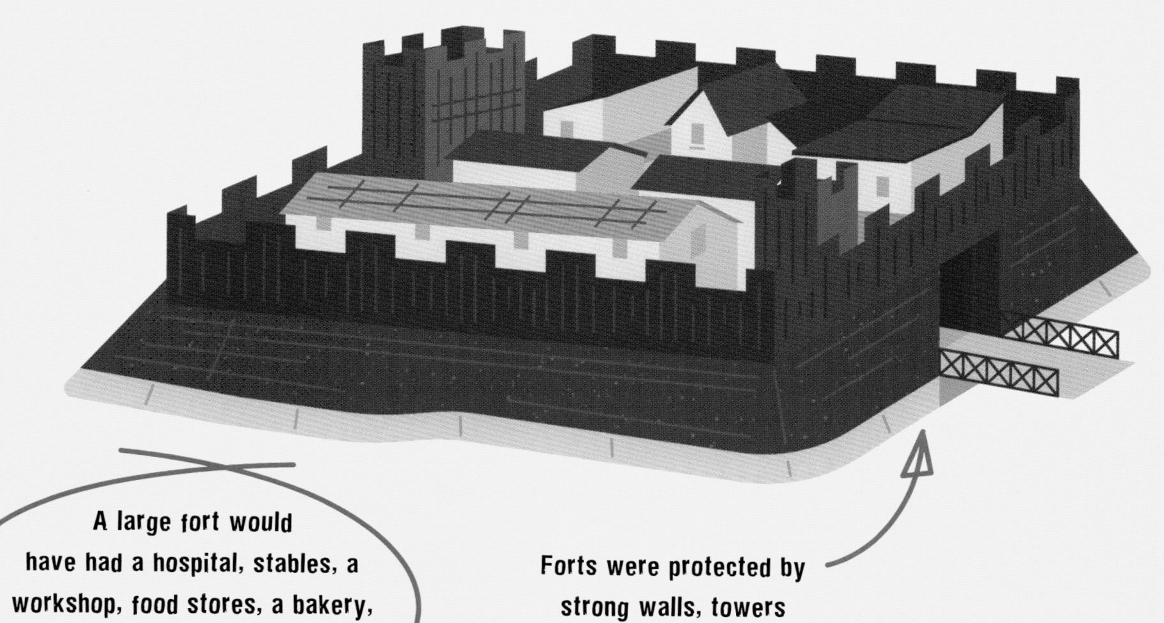

A large fort would have had a hospital, stables, a workshop, food stores, a bakery, a bath-house and public toilets.

Forts were protected by strong walls, towers and ditches.

Soldiers lived in cramped quarters, with eight men to a room, and eighty men to a block.

Life could be hard for the soldiers. They lived far away from home, in basic conditions, for many years.

Engineering, art and architecture

The Romans were superb architects and engineers, who built grand buildings and a network of roads all over their empire – some of which still survive today. Their amazing technical innovations included arches, aqueducts, concrete and even the first central heating system! They were skilled artists and craftspeople, too. Influenced by Greek art, Romans produced many beautiful sculptures, frescoes and mosaics.

Glossary

amphitheatre A large round or oval building, surrounded by tiers of seats, in which **gladiator** contests and other public entertainments were held.

aqueduct A system designed to carry water from one place to another, involving huge arched bridges, channels in the ground and underwater tunnels.

atrium The central courtyard of a Roman house.

emperor The supreme leader of the Roman Empire. Sometimes, the emperor was even thought of as a god.

Empire Either the post-**republican** period in Rome's history, when it was ruled by an **emperor**, or the territory conquered and administered by Rome.

forum The main, central area of a city, where **citizens** would come to meet, do business, and buy and sell goods. The forum was surrounded by important buildings such as temples and government buildings.

fresco A painting done on wet wall plaster. Frescoes decorated the walls of wealthy townhouses and country villas.

gladiators Men (and sometimes women) trained to fight against each other or against wild animals at public shows held in the **amphitheatre.** There were different types of gladiators, each using different weapons and armour.

insulae Multi-storey apartment blocks where Rome's poorer citizens lived. They were often dirty and overcrowded.

latrine A toilet; most Romans relied on communal public latrines.

legionary A soldier aged under 45, who was a Roman **citizen.**

mosaic A picture or pattern made from small pieces of stone or ceramic.

ore A rock containing metal that is valuable enough to be mined.

sculpture A three-dimensional (3-D) figure or design carved from stone, wood, clay or another material.

Senate A governing body, which was made up of important or wealthy members of Roman society. The Senate's role was to debate policy, propose new laws and offer advice to elected officials.

Roman technology

... in 30 seconds

The Romans learned a lot from other cultures, copying the skills and techniques that they wanted for themselves – as well as developing their own. Their technical abilities helped them to become one of history's most powerful and influential civilizations.

Metal-workers used gold, silver, copper, tin, lead, iron and mercury from mines in Britain, Spain and Portugal to produce tools, weapons, nails, coins and fine jewellery. They hammered copper into thin sheets, or heated other ores, such as iron ore, to extract the pure metal. By heating metals into a molten (liquid) form, they could then shape them, using moulds and casts.

Roman glassworkers were masters of their trade – some of their techniques are still not understood! For example, they made vases using different layers of coloured glass. They somehow managed to carve away the top layers to make 'relief' pictures on the surface, called cameos.

All over the Empire, construction projects relied on a new Roman invention – strong, waterproof concrete. It was much easier to transport than heavy blocks of stone, plus it was cheap, easy to use and could be laid in any shape.

3-second sum-up

Skilled workers borrowed from other cultures and also invented their own techniques.

3-minute mission Make jewellery

You need: • Aluminium foil • Coloured beads or plastic gems

1 Cut the foil into large squares, then fold the squares in half, so that you have a thicker sheet to work with.

2 Twist, fold and combine your foil sheets into a decorative bracelet, necklace, brooch or badge.

3 Add the finishing touches to your jewellery by sticking on coloured beads or plastic gems.

Coins, jewellery and tools were made by skilled metal-workers.

The Romans heated ores to extract metals, which could then be worked into different shapes.

A bellows pumps air into the fire, making it burn hotter.

The metal is heated in a crucible on a fire.

The crucible is removed from the fire when the metal is molten (semi-liquid).

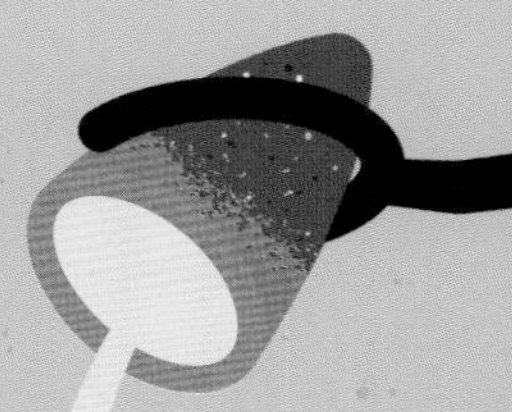

The molten metal is poured into a clay mould, and left to cool.

Jewellery, such as this bracelet, would have been hammered into shape.

Many different types of metal were used, but iron was the most important for making tools.

Building roads

... in 30 seconds

Have you ever heard the saying, 'all roads lead to Rome'? In fact, Rome was the centre of a road network that stretched to the furthest corners of the Empire. Roads were very important to the survival of the Roman civilization, as they helped Romans to move troops, goods and supplies around the Empire.

The roads were built as straight as possible so that people and goods could travel with more ease. They were simple to navigate and had milestones to show distances. They were even designed with rest stops, where horses could be fed and watered, and weary travellers could take a break and eat. Roads were also patrolled by troops, to keep travellers safe.

These highways were built over an 800-year period by legionaries as they marched across the Empire. Some of the roads were simple trackways covered in gravel or crushed rubble, but the major highways were built to last and paved with stone. A major Roman road was built up in layers, with each layer doing an important job. Some of these roads were so well built that they are still intact today, 2,000 years later. Maybe you've travelled on them!

3-second sum-up

The Romans built a vast network of roads, many of which lasted for thousands of years.

The road to battle

You can still see the Via Appia (Appian Way) just outside Rome today. Started in around 312 BCE, the road allowed Roman troops to travel to the city of Capua, 190 km (118 miles) south of Rome, where they were fighting the tribes of Samnium. It was expensive to build, but the Senate agreed that roads like this were vital. Without them, the Roman legions couldn't get around quickly enough to defend the Empire's cities and borders.

Building roads across the Empire was a great way to keep the Roman soldiers busy and useful in times of peace!
The top layers of the road had curved 'cambers' to allow the rainwater to run off to the sides.
Side ditches or stone channels were made, to carry the rainwater away from the roads.
First, the legionaries dug a ditch.
Then they added layers of sand, rubble, crushed stone and stone.

Running water

... in 30 seconds

Roman towns and cities needed huge amounts of fresh water for drinking, washing, cooking – and for flushing away waste. To help transport the water from natural springs, the Romans built aqueducts. These long structures carried flowing water – slightly downhill – over many kilometres. For most of the length, the water flowed in tunnels.

Over time, 11 different aqueducts were built in Rome. Together, they provided the city with more than 750 million litres (200 million gallons) of water each day. Some of the water was stored in giant cisterns (tanks) and delivered to buildings through systems of pipes; other water streamed directly from fountains. This water supply was enough for a city of up to one million people.

Roman engineers also built giant drainage channels under their cities to carry away dirt and sewage, and to prevent settlements from flooding. Even the poorer citizens could keep their homes free of human waste by visiting the public latrines or emptying their toilet pots into the large sewers.

The Roman system was so famous that today we still use a Latin-based word – plumbing – to describe the systems that supply water to our homes. This comes from 'plumbum', meaning 'lead' – the metal the Romans used to make water pipes.

3-second sum-up

Aqueducts, channels and plumbing systems delivered water and took away waste.

Public toilets

Roman public toilets were called 'foricae'. They could fit up to 20 people, on two long benches with holes cut out of the top of them. There was no privacy – in fact, public toilets were seen as a place to chat and catch up on gossip. Instead of toilet paper the Romans used a 'spongia', a sponge on a long stick. This would be rinsed after it was used and put back for the next person to use!

Fresh water was piped into the cities through aqueducts. Waste was carried away through a system of sewers.

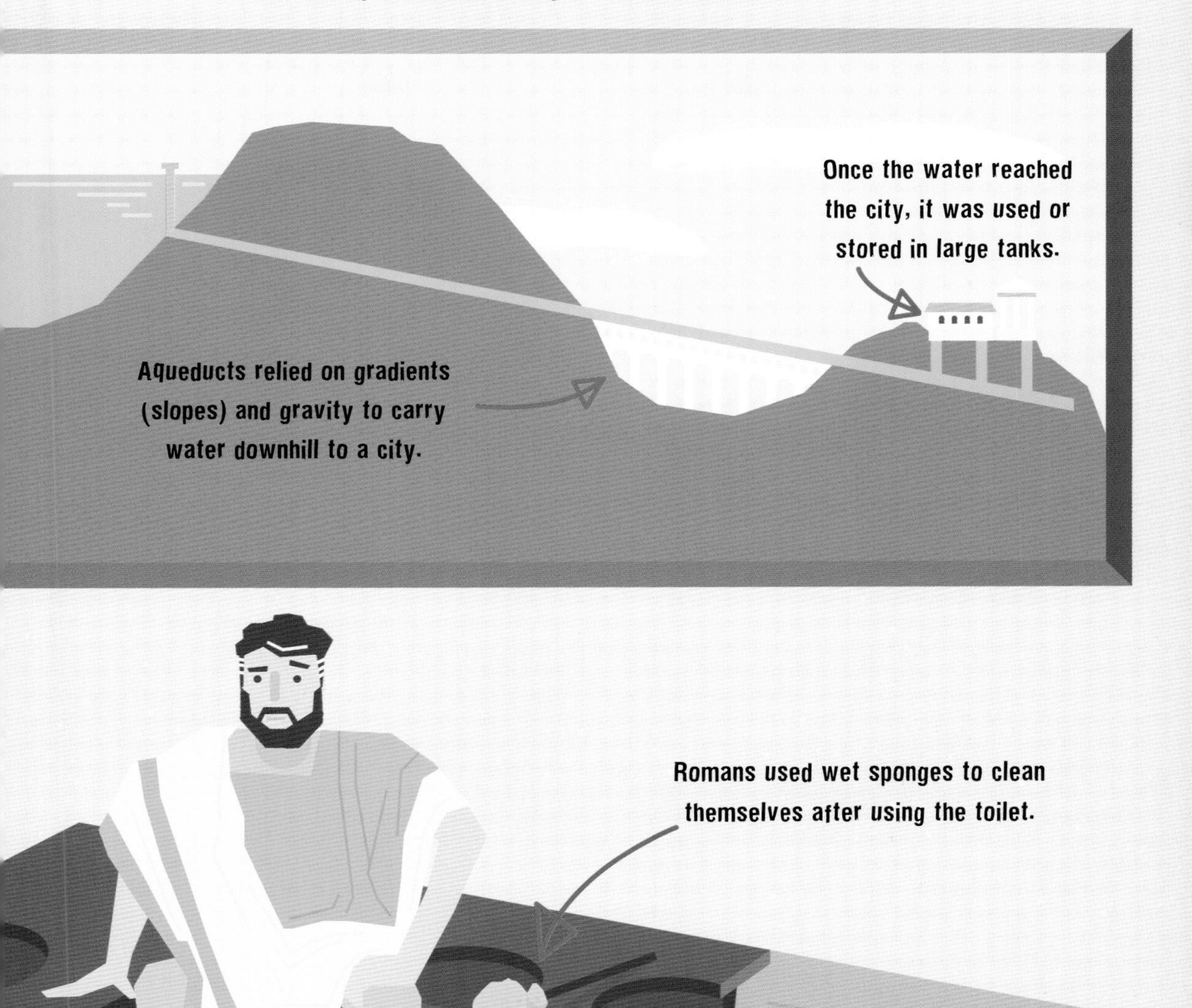

Once the water reached the city, it was used or stored in large tanks.
Aqueducts relied on gradients (slopes) and gravity to carry water downhill to a city.
Romans used wet sponges to clean themselves after using the toilet.

Waste water flowed into the sewer channels, which emptied it into a stream or river.

Ambitious architects

... in 30 seconds

The Romans were ingenious architects, who built on a vast scale all over the Empire. They constructed grand buildings where politicians could meet, as well as temples, bath-houses and theatres for the public, and massive monuments to show off their fame and power.

Roman engineers also loved arches. They realized that a building with arches was just as strong as one made of solid walls, and sometimes even stronger, since arches could span a greater distance and carry more weight than a straight piece of stone. Archways used up fewer materials – and allowed people and vehicles to pass through!

The Romans also worked out how to make huge domes out of concrete. One of the most famous domes in the world forms the roof of a temple called the Pantheon, in Rome. Almost 2,000 years after it was built, it remains the world's largest unreinforced concrete dome.

3-second sum-up

Skilled architects and clever engineers constructed the Empire's great buildings.

3-minute mission Build an arched bridge

You need: • Toilet roll tubes • Cardboard • Scissors • Sticky tape

1 Cut each toilet roll tube in half lengthways, to make two arch shapes. Use as many tubes as you like.

2 Attach the ends of the halved tubes together using sticky tape, to create one long arch shape.

3 Cut a long strip of cardboard to cover the entire length of the top of your toilet roll bridge.

4 Tape the cardboard strip along the length of the top of the arch.

5 Now, test the strength of your bridge. Start with lighter objects and then try heavier ones... until your bridge eventually collapses!

The Pantheon was an incredible architectural achievement, and it is still the world's largest unreinforced concrete dome.

The Pantheon was a temple, but it was probably also used for the emperor's public appearances.

Amazingly, no metal rods or chains were used to support the huge spherical (ball-shaped) dome.

An 'oculus' (a circular hole) forms an opening to the heavens.

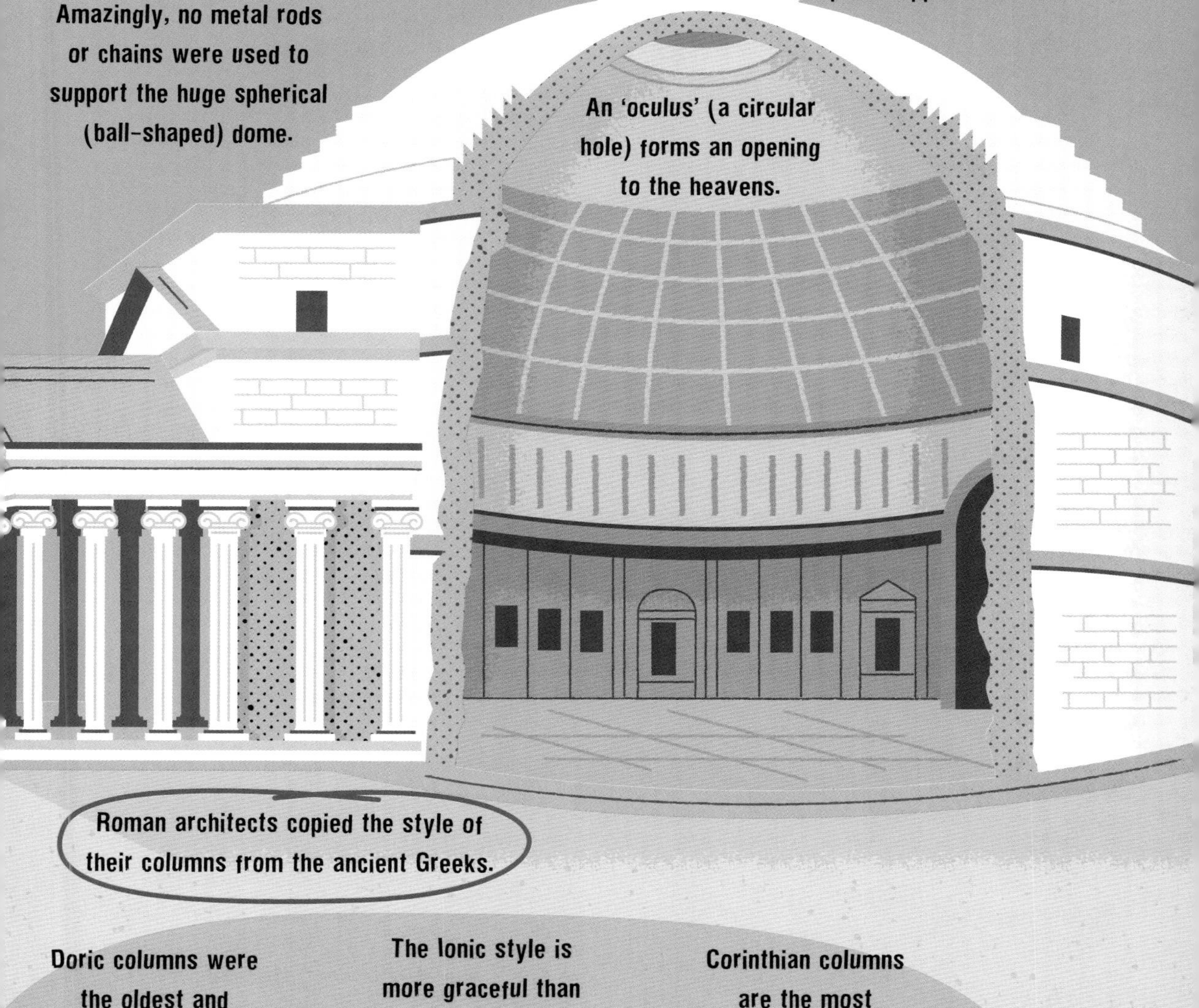

Roman architects copied the style of their columns from the ancient Greeks.

Doric columns were the oldest and simplest style.

The Ionic style is more graceful than the Doric.

Corinthian columns are the most decorative.

Roman homes

... in 30 seconds

Houses and apartments were as varied as our homes are today. Some were grand and beautifully constructed. Others were poorly or cheaply built ... it depended on who lived in them!

In the cities, poorer citizens lived with their families in 'insulae'. These were crowded apartment blocks, usually built on top of shops and public snack bars. Life in these flats could be noisy and dirty. The buildings didn't always have toilets or running water, and because they weren't made of the best materials, they often cracked and crumbled.

Wealthier people lived in townhouses. Here, the rooms were usually built around a central 'atrium' – a paved courtyard area. Rainwater fell through an opening (called a 'compluvium') into a central pool (the 'impluvium'), which kept the air cool in the house. The impluvium also overflowed into a cistern below the ground, so that the water could be stored and used for drinking or cooking.

The Romans even invented a form of central heating, called a 'hypocaust'. Warm air, heated by a furnace, moved around the building in spaces underneath the floors and in hollow bricks in the walls.

3-second sum-up

Rich people's grand houses had heat and water, while the poor lived in small, crowded flats.

Pompeii preserved

When the volcano Mount Vesuvius erupted in 79 CE, it spewed out lava and ash that buried the town of Pompeii for nearly 1,500 years. When it was uncovered in 1748, the city and many of its inhabitants were found perfectly preserved – the volcanic ash that coated everything had hardened, shielding bodies and houses from decay. This important discovery allowed historians to view a snapshot of Roman life.

A townhouse wasn't just a home. It was also an important symbol of wealth and social status.

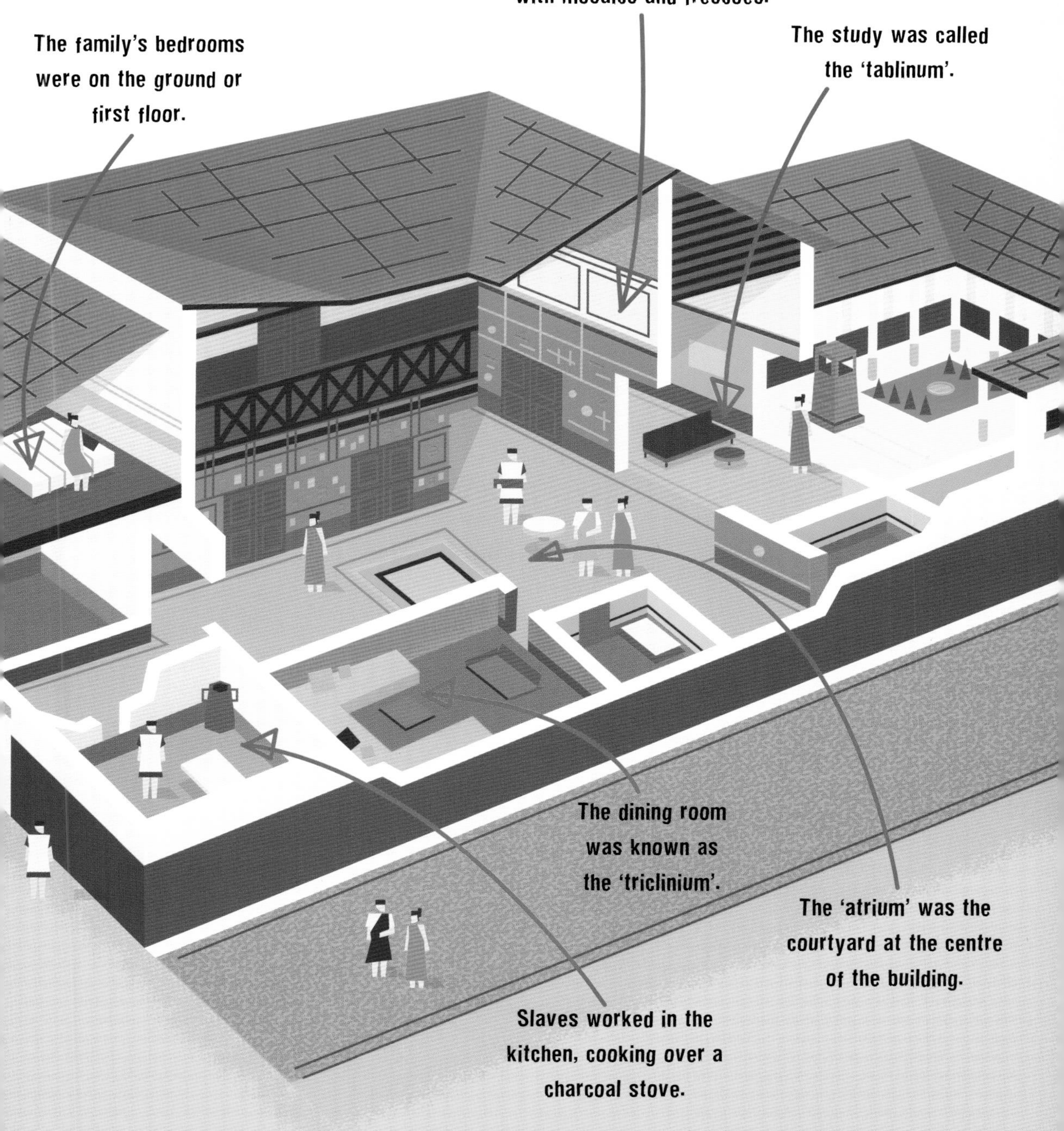

The walls, ceilings and floors were richly decorated with mosaics and frescoes.
The family's bedrooms were on the ground or first floor.
The study was called the 'tablinum'.
The dining room was known as the 'triclinium'.
The 'atrium' was the courtyard at the centre of the building.
Slaves worked in the kitchen, cooking over a charcoal stove.

The city

... in 30 seconds

Roman cities combined luxury and poverty. Elegant public spaces with imposing monuments stood just metres away from a warren of crowded, bustling streets, jammed with shops and 'insulae' (housing for lower-class people).

The central area of most Roman cities, including Rome itself, was the forum. This was an open space where people could meet to trade, do business or talk about politics. The city's main temples and government buildings were clustered around the forum, as a sign of their importance. The main paved streets led away, in a grid pattern, from the forum to the city walls and beyond, through gates guarded by soldiers. The walls protected the city from invasion.

Cities also had places of entertainment that all kinds of citizens could use and enjoy. There were stadiums (called 'circuses') for chariot racing, and large amphitheatres where gladiator fights and other public shows took place. The Colosseum amphitheatre in Rome could probably hold between 45,000 and 50,000 spectators. The emperor paid for these buildings and spectacular events – it was a good way of keeping the public happy!

3-second sum-up

Cities had open public spaces and grand buildings as well as crowded slums.

3-minute mission Town planning

You need: • Paper • Pens and pencils • A ruler

Think about your own town, village or area, and the location of the main buildings and open spaces – for example, your school, the park, the supermarket or shops, the swimming pool and the cinema. Now draw a plan of how YOU would arrange the main places in your town or area. Where would you like your own home to be? And is there anything you would like to add to the plan?

The centre of most cities was a grand public space called the forum.

The forum was surrounded by monuments, government buildings and temples.

Some forums had a platform called the 'rostra', where citizens could stand and give speeches to the crowd. The speakers were called 'orators'.

People gathered at the forum to discuss politics, do business or shop at the markets.

Great art

... in 30 seconds

The Romans were brilliant artists and craftspeople. They excelled at mixing the art and architecture of other cultures into their own style and producing high-quality artworks, many of which still survive today – from delicate ceramics to monumental sculptures.

Sculptures were highly prized and the Romans would create statues of the most famous citizens to show their power and status. The statues sometimes had 'removable' heads though, in case the person became unpopular. The sculpted head of a new hero could then be added in its place!

The Romans painted on a variety of materials, such as wood or ivory, but the paintings that have survived the best are frescoes. These bright and beautiful works of art were painted onto wall plaster. Walls and floors were also decorated with mosaics. These were created using tiny, coloured stones called 'tesserae' that the artists built up into patterns, portraits and scenes from mythological stories. The artists, known as mosaicists, each had their own styles, patterns and favourite subjects.

3-second sum-up

The Romans developed a distinctive artistic style, seen in sculpture, painting and mosaics.

3-minute mission Create a mosaic self-portrait

You need: • Colourful paper (old magazines, plain or tissue paper, foil) • Large paper or card sheet • Pencil • PVA glue

1 Cut or tear the paper into lots of small pieces.

2 Draw the outline of your face onto the card or paper sheet. Add outlines of your eyes, ears, mouth, nose and hair.

3 Arrange your mosaic pieces on the paper to build up your portrait. When you're happy with the picture, glue the pieces in place.

Fresco painters added colours, in layers, to wet plaster.
The best-known Roman art styles are fresco painting, sculpture and mosaics.
Sculptures were carved out of a block of solid marble, and then painted. Some were made from bronze.
Coloured stones were laid in wet cement to make a mosaic floor.

Life and leisure

Daily life in Rome was very different for wealthy Romans and poor commoners. Where you lived, the food you ate, and whether or not you went to school depended on what level of society you belonged to – and if you were a slave you had no rights at all. However, all Roman citizens, even the poorest, were entitled to free entertainment. Chariot racing and gladiator contests, in particular, were very popular.

Life and leisure
Glossary

amphitheatre A large round or oval building surrounded by tiers of seats, in which **gladiator** contests and other public entertainments were held.

citizen A person in Ancient Rome who had certain rights, including the right to elect officials, own property and hold office.

commoner An ordinary Roman of low status and limited wealth.

emperor The supreme leader of the Roman Empire. Sometimes the emperor was even thought of as a god.

Empire Either the post-**republican** period in Rome's history, when it was ruled by an **emperor**, or the territory conquered and administered by Rome.

forum The main, central area of a city, where **citizens** would come to meet, do business, and buy and sell goods. The forum was surrounded by important buildings such as temples and government buildings.

gladiators Men (and sometimes women) trained to fight against each other or against wild animals at public shows held in the **amphitheatre**. There were different types of gladiators, each using different weapons and armour.

legionary A soldier aged under 45, who was a Roman **citizen**.

priest A religious official who was responsible for a temple and the religious events associated with it. A priest would also perform animal sacrifices to the gods.

Senate A governing body, which was made up of important or wealthy members of Roman society. The Senate's role was to debate policy, propose new laws and offer advice to elected officials.

siege When an enemy position is surrounded to ensure that no supplies reach the people trapped within.

stylus A metal 'pen' used for writing on a wax tablet.

Visigoths One of the Germanic or 'barbarian' tribes that battled Rome. Under their leader, Alaric I, they laid siege to Rome in 408 CE, and captured it two years later.

Roman society

... in 30 seconds

Society was divided into many different levels. Firstly, you could either be 'free' or a slave. If you were free, you were either a Roman citizen or a non-citizen or foreigner, called a 'peregrinus'. Citizens had more rights and didn't have to pay as many taxes to the government. They were also allowed to wear a toga – a long, woollen garment that was wrapped and folded around the body.

Citizens were also divided into different social classes. The emperor and the senators were in the uppermost, wealthiest class. Senators had the power to command legions and run parts of the Empire. They could also be priests. Next came the equestrians (knights). Then there were the 'common' orders, including the people who worked as farmers, traders and legionaries.

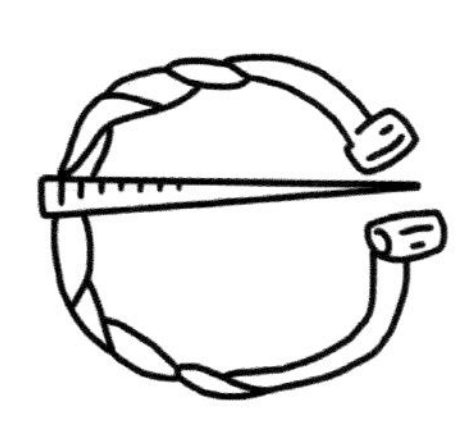

If you weren't free, you were a slave. This meant you could be bought and sold as a servant or labourer. Slaves worked in many places, including farms and mines. Those with the best life were probably the household slaves. They had the chance to build up a good relationship with their masters. At the end of their years of service, some slaves were set free, while others saved up to buy their freedom. They became 'freedmen', or ex-slaves.

3-second sum-up

People were divided into different classes and had different rights.

Roman women

In Roman life, women did not enjoy the same rights as men. Very few girls received an education, and woman were not allowed to be emperors, to serve in the Senate or the army, or to work in government. Unless they had a very high status, they normally had domestic duties (in the home) and remained under the power of their father, even after marriage. However, women were allowed to inherit their parents' property, which meant that some of them were able to own property and start their own businesses.

The way people dressed showed which social class they belonged to.
Citizen – wearing a toga was a sign that you were a Roman citizen.
Emperor – he was allowed to wear the 'trabea' toga, which was mainly purple.
Senator – the colour purple indicated a higher social rank.
Slave – men wore a short tunic in a coarse, dark material.
Equestrian – knights wore tunics with narrow, crimson stripes.
Woman of high status – wealthy women's clothes were dyed in bright colours.

Childhood

... in 30 seconds

The children of ancient Rome were allowed to have fun, but preparing to be an adult was a priority. They respected their elders and were obedient to the 'paterfamilias' (father of the family).

A child born into the slave class would follow in the footsteps of his or her parents, often learning how to perform the same skills and trades, or working for the same masters. Children of ordinary citizens were apprenticed – sent to learn a trade such as weaving, or tanning (preparing leather) from a skilled master – from the age of ten years. Some went to street schools with other children.

Children from a noble family had a better chance of being educated, especially if they were boys. A slave might serve as a 'pedagogus' (teacher), taking the children to a school or instructing them at home. The main subjects were history, maths and literature – but first of all, the pupils had to learn how to read and write in Latin. Pupils learnt by repeating things over and over again.

But Roman children played as well. They had dolls, spinning tops, marbles and wooden animals on wheels, and played board games with dice or pebbles.

3-second sum-up

Children had to learn skills or go to school, but they did have time to play.

Learn some Latin

Ad hoc – 'For this purpose'
Ad infinitum – 'On and on forever'
Carpe diem! – 'Seize the day!'
Per annum – 'For each year'
Post scriptum (often 'P.S.' on a letter) – 'Written later'
Quid pro quo – 'One thing for another thing'
Tempus fugit – 'Time flies'
Veni, Vidi, Vici – 'I came, I saw, I conquered'
Vice versa – 'The positions reversed'

The male children of the rich were taught by tutors or in schools, and had more time to play. Poorer children were often apprenticed to a trade.

Children played games such as marbles.

The 'pedagogus' was a slave who took responsibility for wealthy boys' education.

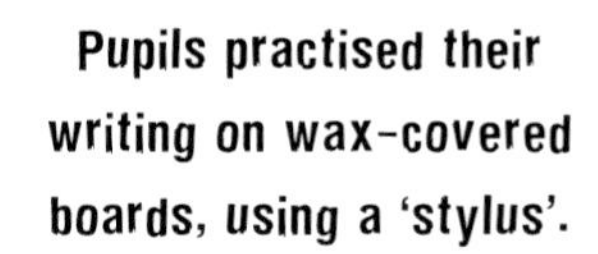

Pupils practised their writing on wax-covered boards, using a 'stylus'.

Feeding the Empire

... in 30 seconds

With its growing population, Rome needed huge and reliable supplies of food. The main crop was wheat, which was ground to make flour for bread. Much of Rome's grain supply came from Egypt and northern Africa. It was vital for Rome to control the Mediterranean Sea to ensure that ships carrying grain arrived safely at Ostia, the port of Rome.

Two other major crops were olives and grapes. Olives were squeezed in presses to make oil, which was transported around the Empire in large vessels, called 'amphorae'. Olive oil was prized for cooking, but was also used in lamps and for washing in public baths. Grapes, grown in vineyards, were also pressed – sometimes by human feet, other times by a machine – and made into wine.

Most people in the Roman world were farmers. Many would have farmed just a few acres, growing cereals, grapes, olives, apples, celery and onions. Many upper-class Romans owned a country villa and adjoining farm. Some of the country estates (called 'latifundia') were very large and specialized in producing certain foodstuffs and livestock for export to the cities. Estates in Spain were famous for their olive oil, while Britain exported woollen goods and beer.

3-second sum-up

Farms all over the Empire supplied cities with staple food such as wheat, olives and wine.

How to starve Rome

When the Visigoths (see pages 86–7) besieged Rome in 408 CE, they occupied the harbour at the mouth of the River Tiber, so that the deliveries of grain from overseas could not get through. Shortly after the siege began, the daily ration of bread (given to each citizen) had to be halved. Then it was reduced to a third. As the weeks went by, people began to starve. The siege worked: after a few months the Senate paid the Visigoths to leave Rome in peace.

Rome needed a reliable supply of food, and plenty of it. When supplies dried up, the angry population rioted!

Supplies were transported up the River Tiber from the port of Ostia.

As well as shipping in food, Rome grew its own crops, including grapes, olives, onions and apples.

RIVER TIBER

OSTIA

Ships laden with wheat, olives and wine criss-crossed the Mediterranean Sea from all parts of the Empire.

Northern Africa was the 'breadbasket' of the Empire, and Rome was dependent on its wheat harvest.

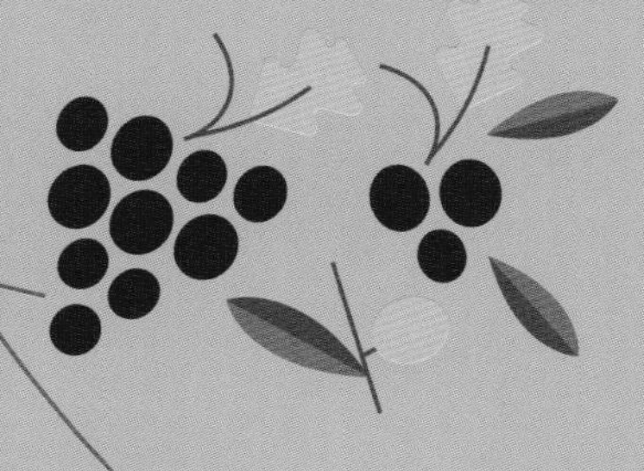

Food and drink

... in 30 seconds

The Romans are famous for their rich diet and lavish feasts. However, the majority of the population ate very simple food and could only dream of the treats served at feasts!

It was difficult to store fresh food, especially in the winter, or if it was being transported over long distances. The Romans developed many ways of preserving food, such as smoking, salting and pickling. If all else failed, they disguised their none-too-fresh ingredients in a salty fish sauce called 'garum'.

On city streets, fast-food bars called 'thermopolia' were owned and run by freed slaves. These sold nourishing stews and porridge, washed down by wine. The bars were popular among poorer people, who didn't have kitchens and running water in their apartments – and they were also great places for meeting up, chatting and exchanging gossip.

Slaves used the busy shops and 'forum' markets to buy the meat, vegetables and oil they needed to cook their wealthy masters' meals. If a slave's master was holding a banquet at his house, several courses, consisting of numerous small dishes, would be served and the shopping list would be huge.

3-second sum-up

For the rich, feasts were luxurious, but most people lived on stews and porridge.

Unusual dishes

Rich Romans liked their food to be experimental. Their slaves served up plates of animal tongues, while the cooks baked dormice or roasted ostriches, peacocks and the legs of giraffes. One of the more ambitious roasts involved stuffing a chicken inside a duck, the duck inside a goose, and the goose inside a pig – before cooking up the whole lot inside a cow. If the master of the house needed a cold, refreshing drink, he might even send his slaves into the hills to fetch snow for making a flavoured 'slushy'.

A banquet would have included all of the finest foods and wines from around the Empire.

The wine was mixed with water to make it weaker.

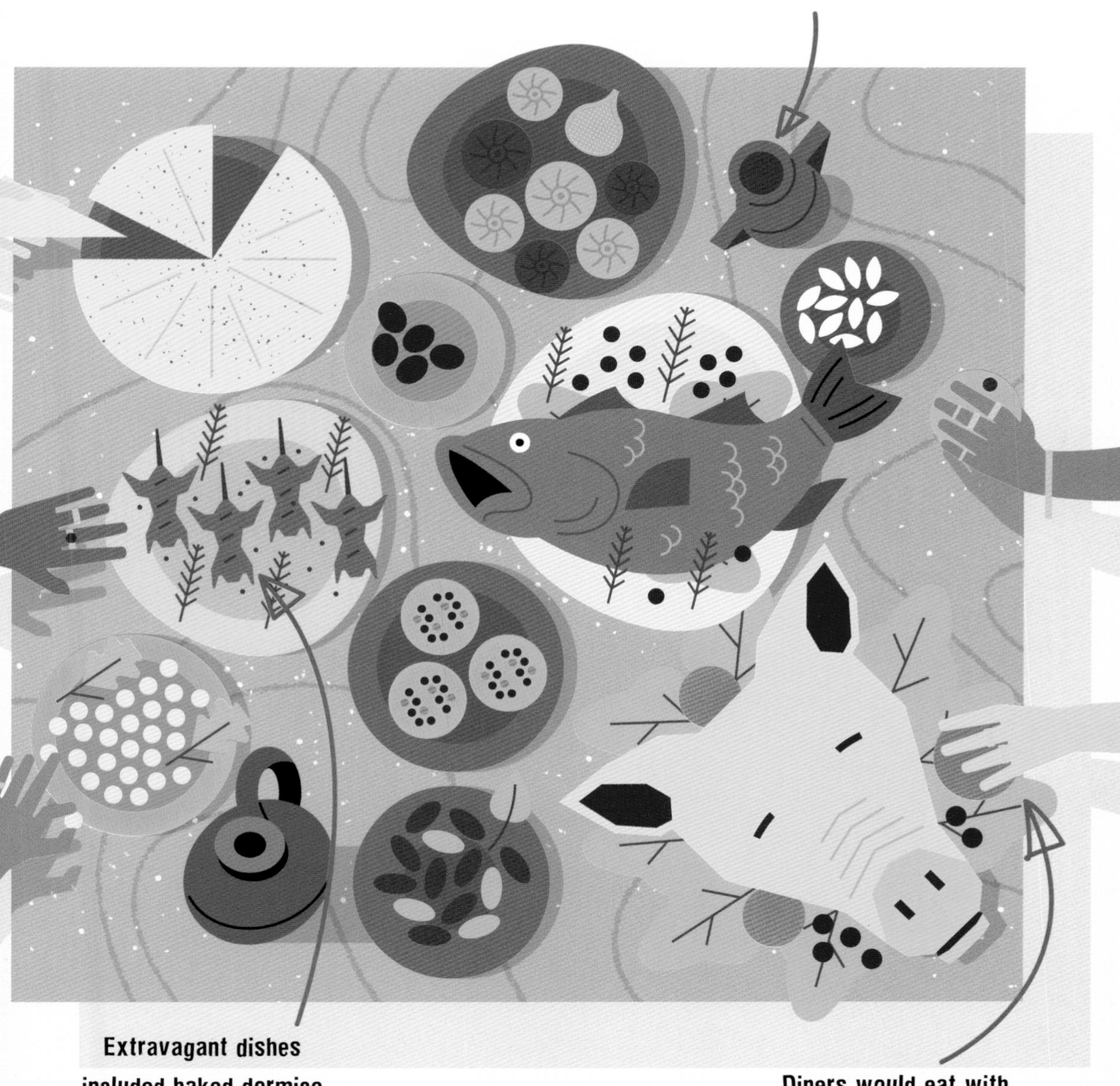

Extravagant dishes included baked dormice and roasted giraffe legs.

Diners would eat with their hands. They lounged on couches that were positioned around the table.

To the baths!

... in 30 seconds

The public baths, known as 'thermae', were an important part of Roman culture. Visiting the baths was a great way to stay happy and healthy, and people often met up with friends and business partners there. Male and female bathers visited at different times and some of the larger bath-houses had separate areas for men and women.

The bathing process lasted several hours. Usually, a bather would do some exercise in the 'palaestra' (an outside gym) before a slave gave him or her a massage with perfumed oils. The slave might also clean the bather's skin by coating it with oil, which was then scraped off using a curved blade called a 'strigil'.

Bathers then had a choice: they could go for a dip in the 'natatio' (cold swimming pool) or enter a 'tepidarium' (warm room). After the warm room, they went to the 'caldarium' (hot room), where they could let their bodies sweat, before soaking in a hot pool. The final room was the 'frigidarium' (cold room), which contained a large, cold plunge pool.

This wasn't the end of the bath-house experience – the rest of the visit was spent at snack bars, walking in the ornate gardens, listening to a poet, watching an acrobat or playing dice games with pals.

3-second sum-up

Roman baths were used for getting clean, relaxing, exercising and doing business.

Healthy Romans

We know about Roman medicines and health treatments from Romans who were writing at the time. Unwashed wool was coated in honey and rubbed into cold sores, or dipped in wine or vinegar to treat a wound. Roman doctors also made medicinal pills using ingredients they could gather from the Mediterranean region. These included onions, carrots, parsley, cabbage, alfalfa, hawthorn, hibiscus and chestnut.

Going to a bath-house was very similar to visiting a modern health spa or leisure centre.
Start off in the dressing room and get changed into a 'subligaculum' (cloth shorts).
Go for a jog, do some stretching or lift some weights in the gym yard.
Enter the saunas (sweat rooms) or go into the 'tepidarium'.
Have a relaxing massage.
Now freshen up in the 'frigidarium'. Use the splash basins to have a wash.

Entertainment

... in 30 seconds

Most of Rome's citizens were in the poorer classes, so the emperor made sure that every person got a monthly ration of grain and free entertainment. A poet called Juvenal summed up these gifts as 'bread and circuses'. They not only kept the common people happy, but also contributed to Rome's reputation as a great empire.

Like many things in their culture, the Romans borrowed their types of theatre from the ancient Greeks. People went to theatres to see comedies, pantomimes and tragedies, or to hear poets recite their work. We know that wealthy people enjoyed theatre, as they added scenes from plays to the decorations inside their houses.

The Circus Maximus, in Rome, was a vast racing track where up to 255,000 sports fans could watch teams of famous charioteers racing against each other. A Roman chariot was a two-wheeled cart pulled by up to four horses, at very dangerous speeds.

Bloodthirsty gladiator contests were also hugely popular. Gladiators were trained to fight in different styles, using weapons and armour. If you went to see a gladiator show at an amphitheatre, you might also see a beast hunt, in which fighters battled with exotic animals, such as lions and bears, from all over the Empire.

3-second sum-up

Many types of entertainment were provided for rich and poor people.

Fight to the death

Some gladiator contests involved prisoners of war, who were forced to fight each other to the death. Slaves were also made to fight as gladiators, but some people become gladiators by choice. They would train hard to become skilled, unbeatable fighters. Many fights were not to the death. If there was a stalemate the emperor might ask the crowd to decide who should be killed and who should be let go.

Different types of gladiators, often from different countries, fought each other to entertain huge crowds.
A Bestiarius would fight a lion or bear or another wild animal.
A Hoplomachus was matched with a Murmillo. The Murmillo had a larger shield, and a sword rather than a spear.
The Secutor was specially trained for fights against the 'net man', Retiarius.

Ideas and beliefs

The Romans were great thinkers. They produced many famous historians, poets and philosophers. Religion was an important part of Roman life. People believed in many gods and goddesses, and were very superstitious, always looking out for good or bad 'omens', or signs from the gods. Around 380 CE, Christianity became the official religion of the Empire and the old forms of Roman religion gradually disappeared.

Ideas and beliefs

Glossary

altar A platform or mound used for animal sacrifices.

amphitheatre A large round or oval building surrounded by tiers of seats, in which **gladiator** contests and other public entertainments were held.

astrology The study of how the position and movement of stars and planets supposedly influences human lives.

convert To change a religious outlook, and adopt another spiritual belief.

emperor The supreme leader of the Roman Empire. Sometimes, the emperor was even thought of as god.

empire Either the post-**republican** period in Rome's history, when it was ruled by an **emperor**, or the territory conquered and administered by Rome.

epic A long, impressive story told through poetry, often about a hero's adventures.

magistrate An official who was elected by the citizens of Rome to serve the Roman government. When Rome was a republic, the **Senate** issued advice to the magistrates, who discussed it and decided whether or not to act on it.

mythological Relating to myths – traditional stories that are not true, and often involve a hero, gods and goddesses, and supernatural events.

omen An event or natural occurrence that is seen as a sign of good or bad fortune to come.

philosopher A person who discusses ideas about the meaning of life.

priest A religious official who was responsible for a temple and the religious events associated with it. A priest would also perform animal sacrifices to the gods.

province An area under the control of another country.

Senate A governing body, which was made up of important or wealthy members of Roman society. The Senate's role was to debate policy, propose new laws and offer advice to the elected officials.

shrine A place within the home that contained statues of gods and spirits, which the family would pray to.

superstition A belief in the supernatural (for instance, ghosts, witches, bad **omens**) that is not based on reason.

Big ideas

... in 30 seconds

The Romans, influenced by the Ancient Greeks, thought deeply about the world, and expressed their ideas through poetry, history, philosophy and literature. Many of their ideas are still discussed and valued today.

One of the most famous poets was called Virgil (70–19 BCE). He wrote an epic Latin poem called *The Aeneid* that was so epic, he never finished it! The poem tells the story of a mythological hero called Aeneas who became the ancestor of the Roman people.

Other writers wanted to tell the real history of the Romans. Livy (59 BCE–17 CE) wrote an enormous set of books about the foundation of Rome. But perhaps the greatest Roman historian was Tacitus (56–c.120 CE). He described – in incredible detail – the reigns of Rome's first emperors, as well as the Germanic tribes beyond the Empire's borders.

Seneca the Younger (c.4 BCE–65 CE) and Marcus Aurelius (121–180 CE) were famous 'Stoic' philosophers. They believed that the world was chaotic and beyond our control, but that we CAN control our own thoughts and beliefs, and therefore be 'good' people.

3-second sum-up

Roman thinkers built on Greek traditions to become famous poets, philosophers and historians.

3-minute mission Expand your big ideas

It's your turn to be a philosopher! What are YOUR big ideas? Is there a question that you want to get to the bottom of? Write down one of your questions, and then spend three minutes either talking or writing about it. Two examples are 'Should we care about the environment?', and 'Is it better to try to be a good person?' Try to explain the reasoning behind your decision.

Some Roman writers studied ancient poetry and philosophy. Others were statesmen who also became great writers or historians.

PLINY THE ELDER: 23–79 CE
Pliny's work inspired the kind of encyclopedias that people still use today.

VIRGIL: 70–19 BCE
Virgil was a writer who loved to blend mythological stories with the history of Rome.

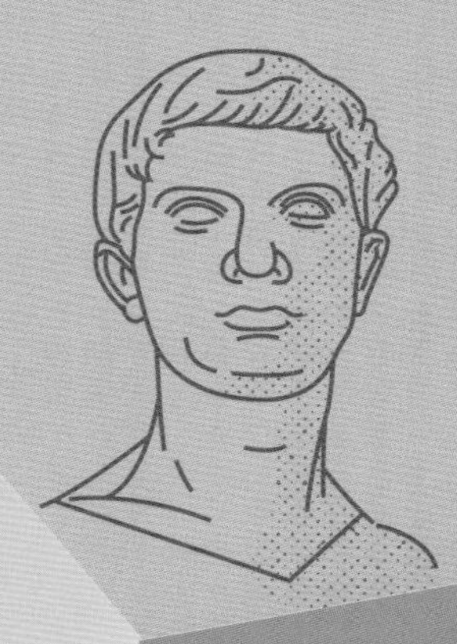

LIVY: 59 BCE–17 CE
Much of what we know about the Romans comes from the work of historians such as Livy.

MARCUS AURELIUS: 121–180 CE
Marcus Aurelius served as emperor in 161–180 CE, but was also a famous philosopher.

Superstition and fortune

... in 30 seconds

The Roman people had a very strong belief in fortune-telling and the supernatural. Certain events or natural happenings were seen as 'omens' (signs) of either good or bad fortune to come. This belief that natural phenomena could predict the future was probably adopted from the Etruscans.

People who told the future and interpreted what the signs meant were called 'augurs' and soothsayers. Any natural disaster was seen by them as a sign that the gods were angry and needed to be pleased. They also used tools, such as the patterns made by flying birds, or the entrails from human or animal sacrifices, to help them.

If the omens weren't good, emperors and generals would sometimes delay their actions, such as marching into battle. Other emperors would not begin their daily routines until they had talked to a soothsayer. Emperor Claudius established a college of soothsayers to protect this tradition.

People wore amulets, or lucky charms, to ward off bad spirits such as the 'evil eye'. This was when a demon, ghost, evil spirit or witch looked at you in a certain way, which could make you sick, cause an accident or give you some other form of bad luck.

3-second sum-up

Romans believed that the future could be predicted, and were very superstitious.

Superstition and monsters

To a Roman, something as normal as spilling wine was thought to be a bad omen. Other disastrous signs were a cockerel crowing during a party, a black cat entering the house or a snake falling from the roof. People believed in evil spirits such as werewolves, vampires and old women who could turn into birds, while children were terrified of the Lamia and the Mormo, which sucked children's blood.

People believed in omens (signs from the gods), astrology and evil spirits.

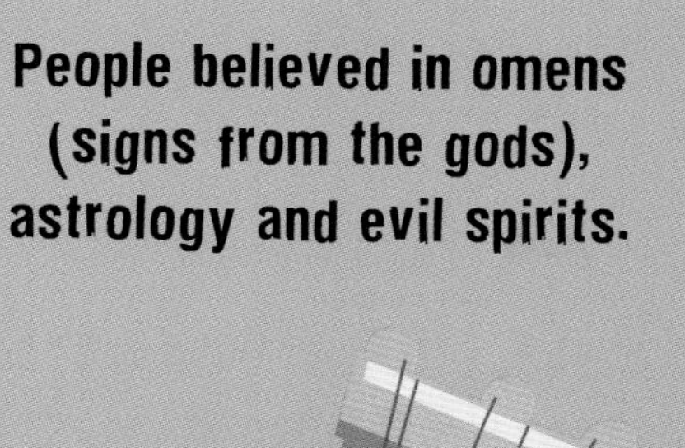

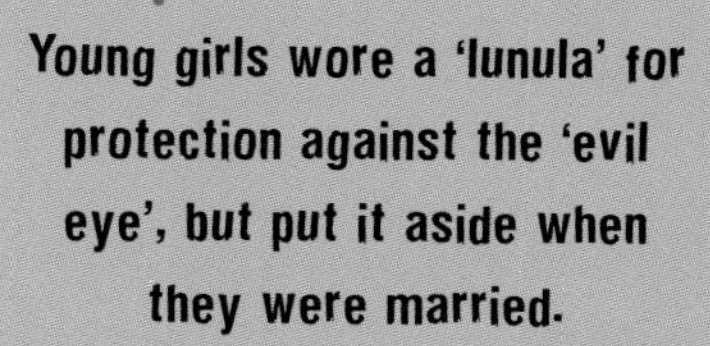

Young girls wore a 'lunula' for protection against the 'evil eye', but put it aside when they were married.

Young boys wore a 'bulla' around the neck as a locket to protect against bad spirits.

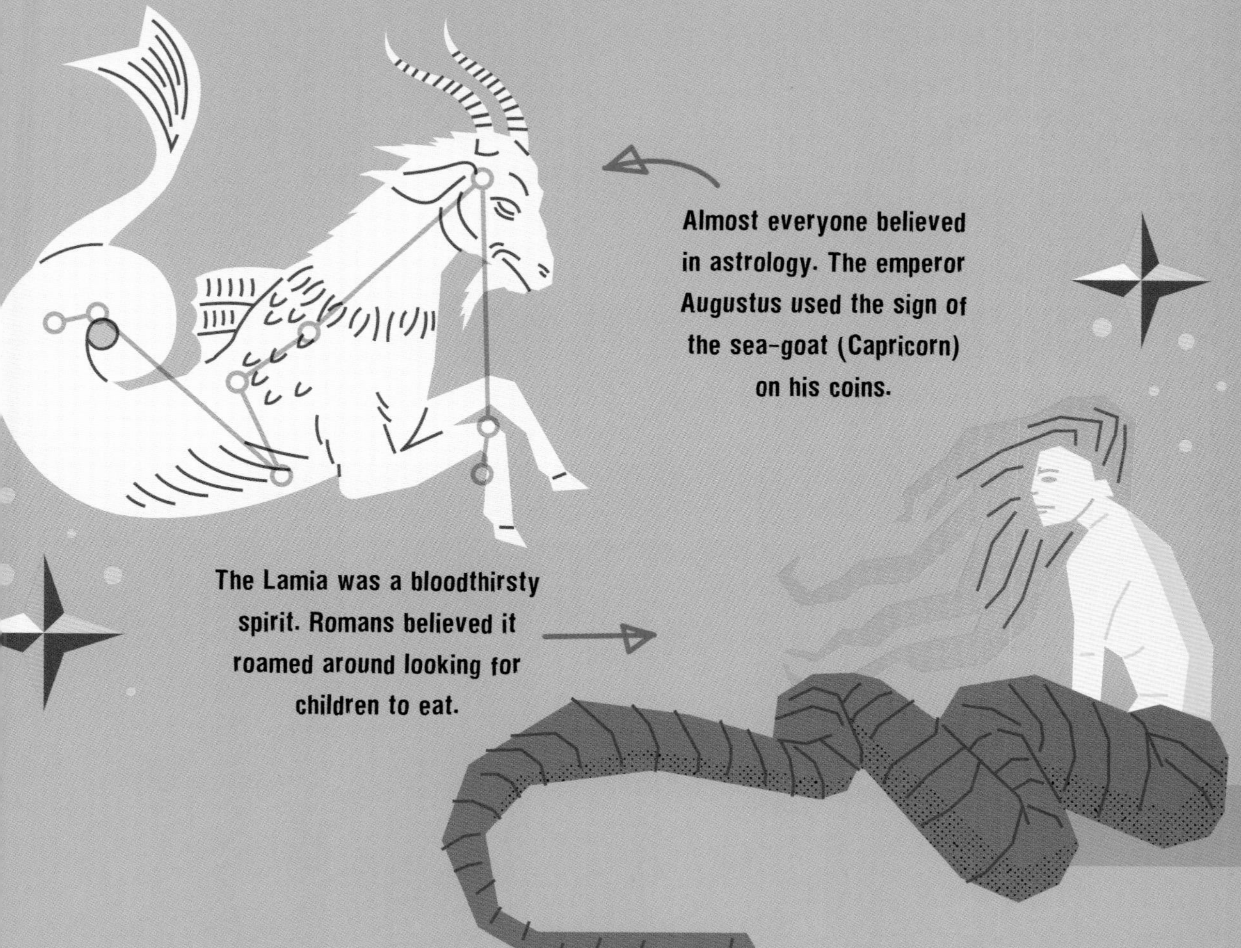

Almost everyone believed in astrology. The emperor Augustus used the sign of the sea-goat (Capricorn) on his coins.

The Lamia was a bloodthirsty spirit. Romans believed it roamed around looking for children to eat.

Gods and goddesses

... in 30 seconds

Roman religion blended lots of different traditions, rituals, ideas and superstitions together. As the Empire expanded, the Romans also 'borrowed' beliefs, traditions and gods from the places they'd conquered.

By 146 BCE, parts of what we now call Greece had come under Roman control, and there were also Greek colonies in southern parts of Italy. As the two cultures mixed, the gods and goddesses of the Greek religion were absorbed into the Roman religion. The Romans used old Etruscan or Latin names, though – for example, Zeus (the Greek king of the gods) became Jupiter, while Artemis (the Greek goddess of hunting) was called Diana.

Specific temples were dedicated to the worship of each god, which was called a 'cult', and each cult had its own priests. Different cults became popular at various times. For example, the worship of Mithras, a bull-slaying god, was widespread between the 1st and 4th centuries CE.

There were also hundreds of minor gods and spirits, who looked after every aspect of life, from the weather, nature and farming, to health, luck and prosperity. People had altars and shrines at home, decorated with paintings or statues of these gods, where offerings were made.

3-second sum-up

The many different gods and goddesses were a blend of ideas, beliefs and traditions from other cultures.

Household gods

The Romans had gods for almost everything! Janus was the god of doorways and beginnings, and was the chief guardian of the house. Cardea was the goddess of door hinges, while Limentius was the god of the threshold (the bottom part of a doorway that you cross when entering a room). Vesta was the goddess of the fireplace, the spiritual centre of a Roman home. There was even a god of manure, called Sterculius, and a god of mould known as Robigus.

There were 12 main gods and goddesses.
MERCURY:
The winged messenger
NEPTUNE:
Lord of the sea
MINERVA:
Goddess of the city
VENUS:
Goddess of love and beauty
CERES:
Goddess of corn and harvests
JUPITER:
Lord of the sky
JUNO:
Protector of marriage
APOLLO:
God of the Sun
VESTA:
Goddess of the home and family
MARS:
God of war
LCAN:
f fire and
forge
DIANA:
Goddess of the wild

Religious festivals

... in 30 seconds

The Roman calendar was packed full of religious festivals. These were known as 'feriae' (holy days), and were normally dedicated to one or more gods or spirits. Romans believed that these minor gods and spirits controlled every aspect of life, and the festivals were intended to keep them happy, so that the harvests (and people's health) would be good.

Some of the feriae were held on fixed days of the calendar. For example, Saturnalia was a winter festival held on the week following December 17th. It was quite similar to Christmas, and involved feasting, drinking, visiting friends and exchanging gifts. Other feriae marked special occasions, or even particular threats. For example, the priests or magistrates might announce a holiday if a brilliant military victory had taken place, or if they felt Rome was in grave danger.

Events dedicated to a god, or several gods, often involved a procession to a temple dedicated to them. Prayers were recited, and offerings and animal sacrifices would be made in front of the temple steps. The animal's important organs were often burned, so that the rising smoke would carry the offerings up into the world of the gods. The rest of the animal was eaten later on, at a feast – a tasty barbecue for the people.

3-second sum-up

Festivals and public holidays were held in every single month of the year.

3-minute mission Swapping places

In the festival of Saturnalia, wealthy masters would swap places with their slaves. A slave would wear his master's clothes for the day, and be waited on by him. Imagine YOU could swap places with anyone you wanted for a day. Who would it be, and what would you get up to? Write down what you think your day would be like.

The Saturnalia was a festival held from 17–23 December, dedicated to Saturn, the god of seed-sowing and agriculture.

Sometimes a household master would swap places with his slave for a few days!

Everyone enjoyed feasting, drinking wine and dancing.

People exchanged gifts and greetings on the last day of the festival, known as the Sigillaria.

Christianity arrives

... in 30 seconds

Although Romans believed in many gods, not everyone shared their views. Followers of the Christian religion, started by Jesus of Nazareth from the Roman province of Palestine, believed there was only one true god.

The Roman authorities thought this rejection of their gods and the worship of just one god was deeply suspicious. The early Christians also refused to offer sacrifices to the emperor, a semi-divine monarch. Jesus was crucified (nailed to a cross) outside Jerusalem and, over time, many of his followers were rounded up, tortured and killed.

However, in about 312 CE the emperor Constantine is said to have had a vision the night before a battle, in which Jesus directed him to fight under the sign of the Christian cross. Constantine's victory the next day appeared to justify his faith in the new god, and he converted to Christianity. Christians and pagans were allowed to worship freely, and in 380 CE Christianity became the official religion of the Empire.

Constantine, and the emperors who came after him, assisted the Christian leaders and provided money for churches to be built. Over the next two centuries, more and more Romans turned to Christianity.

3-second sum-up

Christianity became more popular in Rome, after Constantine adopted it as his religion.

Christian Martyrs

Before Constantine's conversion, Roman emperors feared that Christians would damage the relationship between the Roman people and their gods, so Christians were persecuted and executed. As well as being crucified or burned, some were forced to fight to the death in gladiator contests, or were thrown to wild beasts, such as lions. Many Christians were forced to meet and worship in secret.

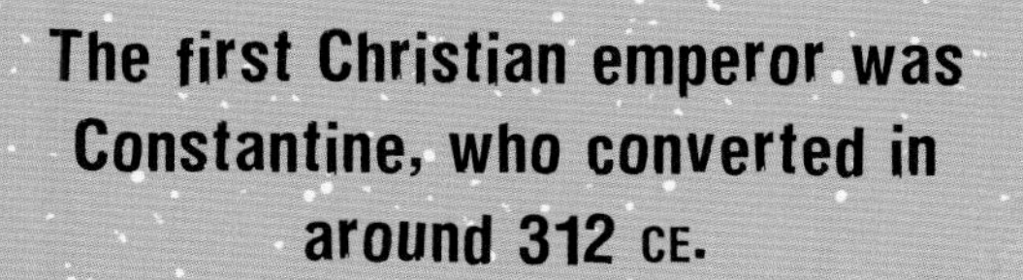

The first Christian emperor was Constantine, who converted in around 312 CE.

The night before a battle, Constantine supposedly dreamt that a cross appeared in the sky, and heard the words 'Under this sign you will win'.

Constantine painted the sign of the Christian cross on his men's shields and won the battle.

Constantine put an end to the mistreatment of Christians, and Christianity eventually became the official religion of the Empire.

End of the Empire

The downfall of the mighty Roman Empire began in the 3rd century CE. Under attack from all sides, it was split into two parts to make it easier to control. The Western Roman Empire struggled on for another 200 years, while the Eastern Roman Empire – known as the Byzantine Empire – lasted until 1453. Many of the Romans' amazing ideas and inventions, from Republican forms of government and drainage systems, to concrete and central heating, are still around today.

End of the Empire

Glossary

emperor The supreme leader of the Roman Empire. Sometimes, the emperor was even thought of as a god.

Empire Either the post-**republican** period in Rome's history, when it was ruled by an **emperor**, or the territory conquered and administered by Rome.

government A group of people who make and administer a country's or territory's laws.

leap year A year with 366 days instead of 365. A leap year occurs every four years.

portico A roof supported by columns, often at the entrance to a building.

Roman numerals The Roman system of numbers, represented by seven different letters: I, V, X, L, C, D and M (representing 1, 5, 10, 50, 100, 500 and 1,000, respectively). Roman numerals are still seen and used today, such as on clock and wristwatch faces.

Senate A governing body, which was made up of important or wealthy members of Roman society. The Senate's role was to debate policy, propose new laws and offer advice to the elected officials.

tribe A group of people with a shared culture and language.

End of the Western Empire

... in 30 seconds

The Roman Empire reached the height of its power in the 2nd century CE. But a century later, it was in big trouble. Its armies were struggling to keep back the forces of the Sassanid (Persian) Empire in the east, and those of the Germanic tribes in northern Europe. The Empire was huge and hard to control. Its emperors were weak and didn't last long – more than 20 ruled in the space of just 75 years.

When an emperor called Diocletian took charge, in 284 CE, his solution was to split the Empire into four different regions to make it easier to govern. The arrangement, of two chief emperors and two 'trainee' emperors, was called the 'Tetrarchy'. This new system would eventually lead to the break up of the Empire into two distinct halves – east and west – in the 4th century.

The Eastern Roman Empire grew in wealth, but the Western Empire had less money, and attacks from the 'barbarian' tribes of northern Europe were gaining in strength. The Romans actually hired fighters from the opposing tribes to help. These warriors were fierce but had little loyalty to the Romans. In 476 CE, Emperor Romulus Augustulus was overthrown by one of their leaders, Flavius Odoacer. The Western Roman Empire was no more.

3-second sum-up

The struggling Empire was eventually split into two, and the western half came to an end.

The barbarians

The term 'barbarians' was used by the Romans to describe anybody who wasn't part of their Empire. There were lots of different barbarian groups, many of them Germanic tribes from northern Europe. They were all very different from each other, and fought each other as well as the Romans. The main tribes were the Goths (the Visigoths and the Ostrogoths), the Franks, the Vandals, the Huns and the Saxons.

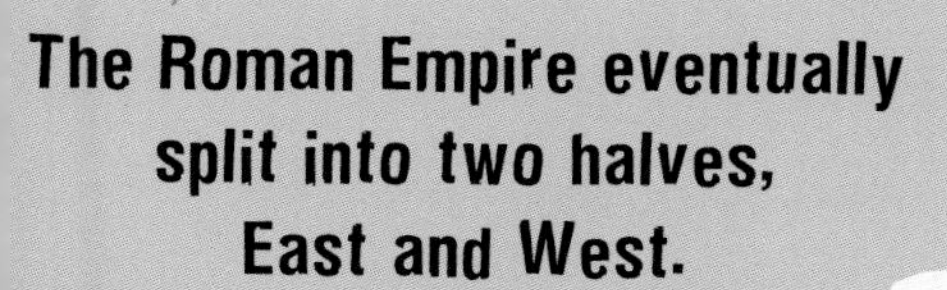

The Roman Empire eventually split into two halves, East and West.

The Western Roman Empire found itself increasingly under attack from 'barbarian' tribes.

Visigoths and other Germanic tribes attacked Rome.

The Huns swept west from Asia, threatening the Germanic tribes and Rome.

WESTERN ROMAN EMPIRE

ROME

CONSTANTINOPLE

EASTERN ROMAN EMPIRE

A Germanic tribe called Vandals attacked in northern Africa and Spain.

The Western Roman Empire came to an end in 476 CE, when it was overthrown by a Germanic tribe.

End of the Eastern Empire

... in 30 seconds

Unlike the Western Empire, the Eastern Roman Empire was well protected, economically successful and had a strong army, so it lasted for almost another 1,000 years after the fall of the Western Empire.

The Emperor Constantine also decided to move the capital from Rome to the Eastern Empire. He built a city called Constantinople – named after himself! – on the old city of Byzantium (in modern-day Turkey).

In the 7th century, an emperor called Heraclius changed the official language of the Empire from Latin to Greek and restored the original Greek name of the capital city: Constantinople became Byzantium again, and the Empire was now known as the Byzantine Empire.

The Empire soon came under attack, first from Arab forces in northern Africa, in 640–98 CE. They later besieged Byzantium itself. Swedish Vikings also attacked the capital city, in the 9th century. The Byzantines held firm against these attacks, but then, in the 11th century, the powerful Seljuk Turks from central Asia began to conquer parts of Byzantium. Finally, in 1453, the Ottoman Turks brought an end to the Byzantine Empire.

3-second sum-up

Rome's successor, the Byzantine Empire, thrived for centuries before falling to the Ottoman Turks.

Who were the Byzantines?

The Byzantines spoke Greek and created a different version of Christianity, called Eastern or Greek Orthodox Christianity. One of the Byzantines' greatest emperors was Justinian. He encouraged art, music and drama, and made lots of reforms, such as allowing women the right to buy land. He also built the Hagia Sophia in Constantinople (now called Istanbul), which is still one of the largest places of worship in the world.

The Eastern Roman Empire – later known as the Byzantine Empire – lasted for over 1,000 years.

313–364 CE

The Roman Empire splits into eastern and western halves.

527–565 CE

The Eastern Roman Empire reaches its greatest power and wealth under Justinian I.

626 CE

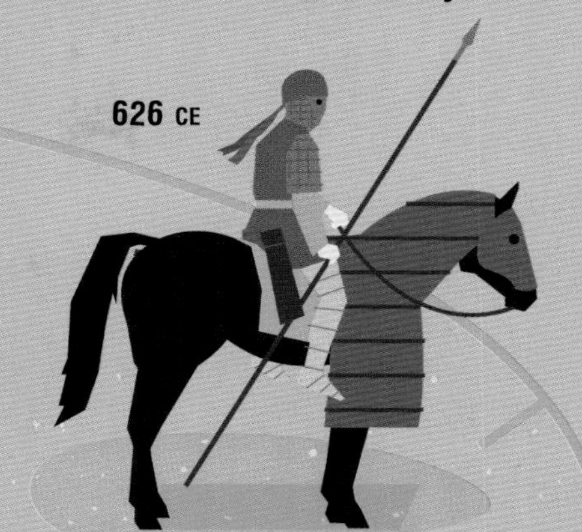

The Byzantine capital city Constantinople is besieged by the Sassanid Persians, Avars and Slavs.

634–41

Arab armies conquer Egypt and the eastern Mediterranean. Later, they take most of northern Africa, too.

1071

Most of Asia Minor (now called Turkey) falls to the Seljuk Turks.

1326–3

The Ottoman Turks win the important cities of Prusa and Nicaea.

1341–1347

The plague known as the 'Black Death' kills millions and further weakens the Empire.

1453

The Ottoman Turks conquer Constantinople, and the Byzantine Empire comes to an end.

The Roman legacy
... in 30 seconds

An amazing number of Roman creations and inventions are still in use today, from concrete and central heating through to Roman numerals. Many modern roads trace the routes carved out by the Romans, and Roman architecture, with its grand columns and porticos, is found in many important public buildings, such as our banks and courthouses.

The Roman idea of piping water (using aqueducts) into cities, for everyday use and hygiene, remains an essential part of town planning today. The Roman invention of a gigantic sewer, which ran under the streets of Rome, is the forerunner of all our modern drainage systems.

Most modern-day democracies follow Roman ideas such as elected leaders, law-making assemblies, and a separate justice system. The Romans gave us many other legal ideas, too, including trial by jury, contracts and wills.

The Romans even invented the modern calendar. In 46 BCE, Julius Caesar brought in reforms, which divided the year into 365 days and 12 months for the first time. He also introduced the idea of the leap year. Finally, many languages have evolved from Latin. These are called the 'Romance' languages, which include French, Spanish and Italian.

3-second sum-up

The ideas and inventions that strengthened the Roman Empire continue to influence the modern world.

Writing history

Whenever the Romans conquered new or 'barbarian' lands, their subjects were introduced to the Roman alphabet. It has gone on to become the most widespread alphabet in the world. Until around the 5th century, the Roman alphabet read from right to left, not left to right. In the classic Roman alphabet, the letters J, U and W were missing, and the letters K, Y and Z were only used for words of Greek origin.

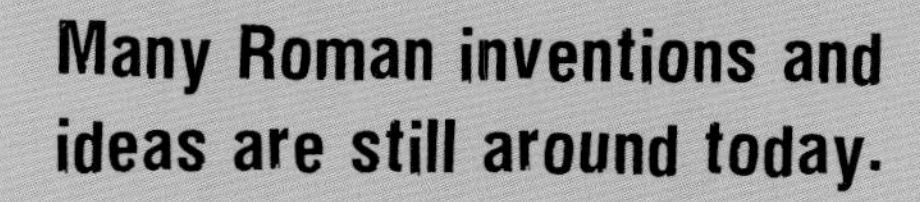

Many Roman inventions and ideas are still around today.

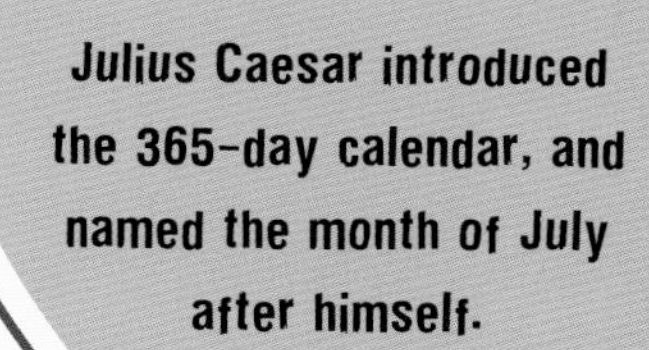

Julius Caesar introduced the 365-day calendar, and named the month of July after himself.

Roman numerals were used in Europe up until the 1600s, when the 'Arabic' numbers we use today took over – but numerals are still sometimes used.

The Romans gave us the idea of trial by jury.

The Roman alphabet is the most-used alphabet in the world.

Discover more

NON-FICTION BOOKS

Horrible Histories
The Rotten Romans
by Terry Deary
Scholastic, 2007

DK Eyewitness Guide: Ancient Rome
by Simon James
Dorling Kindersley, 2011

Through Time: Pompeii
by Richard Platt
Kingfisher, 2007

Ancient Rome: Revealed
by Peter Chrisp
Dorling Kindersley, 2003

The Kingfisher Atlas of the Ancient World
by Simon Adams
Kingfisher, 2006

What They Don't Tell You About... Romans in Britain
by Bob Fowke
Wayland, 2013

Hands on History: Romans
by Fiona MacDonald
QED, 2008

30 Seconds Ancient Rome
by Matthew Nicholls
Ivy Press, 2014

FICTION BOOKS

Diary of Dorkius Maximus
by Tim Collins
Buster Books, 2013

My Story: Pompeii
by Sue Reid
Scholastic, 2015

My Story: Roman Invasion
by Jim Eldridge
Scholastic, 2016

Romans on the Rampage
by Jeremy Strong
Puffin, 2015

APPS

Britannia Kids: Ancient Rome 2014

Ancient Rome for Kids
https://itunes.apple.com/gb/app/ancient-rome-for-kids/id965123536?mt=8

WEBSITES

The British Museum
http://www.britishmuseum.org/learning/schools_and_teachers/resources/cultures/ancient_rome.aspx

BBC Roman Empire
http://www.bbc.co.uk/education/topics/zwmpfg8

DK Find Out
http://www.dkfindout.com/uk/history/

Romans Revealed
http://www.romansrevealed.com

National Geographic Kids
http://www.ngkids.co.uk/history/10-facts-about-the-ancient-Romans

Although every endeavour has been made by the publisher to ensure that all content from these websites is educational material of the highest quality and is age appropriate, we strongly advise that Internet access is supervised by a responsible adult.

DVDs – suitable for all ages

When Rome Ruled
(National Geographic, 2011)

Roman Mysteries
(BBC, 2007)

Index

Index